Memorable Messages

Memorable Messages

The Communications That Stick with Us Over Time

Valerie Rubinsky *and*
Angela Cooke-Jackson

Jefferson, North Carolina

ISBN (print) 978-1-4766-9896-0
ISBN (ebook) 978-1-4766-5770-7

Library of Congress Cataloging-in-Publication Data

Library of Congress Control Number 2025053355

Printed in the United States of America

Toplight is an imprint of McFarland & Company, Inc., Publishers

Box 611, Jefferson, North Carolina 28640
www.toplightbooks.com

To Valerie's mother
and in loving memory of Angela's

Table of Contents

Acknowledgments

Acknowledgments from Val

First and foremost, I want to thank my parents and especially my mom both for permission to share her stories in this book and for a lifetime of wisdom so profound I literally wrote a book about it. I thank my large, loving family for so much support and encouragement over the years. Thank you to my two best friends, Meghan and Dani, for reading earlier drafts of this book and listening to me talk about the idea nonstop for years. And, of course, I thank my spouse Sam, for everything.

To everyone who helped me grow as a writer and social scientist, thank you. That list includes far too many to name but I will name a few: Dr. Angela Hosek, who first introduced me to the idea of memorable messages and who has remained a friend and mentor for more than a decade; my research assistants at the time of the writing of this book, Morgan Cafferata and Callie Tolman, whose feedback helped shape this and many other projects; and our friend and collaborator Jacqueline Gunning, whose work and wisdom contributed significantly to the theory of memorable messages. Lastly, of course, I want to acknowledge my coauthor, friend, writing partner, and mentor, Angela Cooke-Jackson. My life has changed in too many ways to count through knowing you.

Acknowledgments from Angela

I believe strongly in the importance of mentorship and bending into the wise foretelling of the elders and ancestors—those who have passed—in my life. My mother, who passed in 1998, always encouraged me to keep good people, both old and young, in my life, people who could teach me to be malleable and confident, people who could teach me to be proud and also humble, people who could teach me the importance of whimsy and the value of quiet. My mother was an invincible renaissance woman whom I believe was before her time.

I would also like to thank the other women who have imprinted my life—my sister Lynne, who would give the clothes off her back if it were required of her; my aunt Rose, whose quiet persistence taught me patience; and my longtime friend and former college professor Debbie Bush Haffey, whose practical wisdom helped me learn that my dreams were important, but that I needed to be ordered and practical in my journey to obtain them. They all hold space in my body, reminding me of what it means to be grounded, balanced, and conscientious in an ever-shifting culture—to be true to who I am.

I am and have always been my co-author's biggest fangirl. Valerie, you are a quiet, unwavering energy and I strive to have your fortitude and persistence every day.

Preface

Have you ever wondered why certain words or conversations stick with you more readily than others? Or have you ever questioned how those words affect you? What does it mean that you remember that specific conversation or saying? As adults, we often make comments like "My mother used to say to me," "When I was a kid my father always said," or "I grew up hearing...." Why do you think about those messages when you're pondering a new challenge, when you're stressed or anxious, or even when you're elated? Have you ever considered how to make your own communication more memorable or ensure it impacts those you care about in more positive ways? If so, this book is for you.

The concept of memorable messages entered the field of communication research in 1981 through an important research study by Mark Knapp, Cynthia Stohl, and Kathleen Reardon. They began their project with the simple statement "*Some interpersonal messages are reported to be remembered for a long time and to have a profound influence on a person's life.*"[1] We want to acknowledge the decades of memorable message research, published by so many brilliant researchers and writers, that informed our own perspectives and without whom this book would not be possible. Before Val finished elementary school, dozens of research studies explored these memorable messages and their impact on our identity, behavior, and relationships. Many researchers in communication and psychology went on to learn about the nature and function of these messages in too many contexts to list, but most commonly when it comes to messages we receive about health behaviors, sexuality, relationships, school, money, and work.

The two of us came to the study of memorable messages in 2012 when we first met as a graduate student and professor at Emerson College in Boston. Research, both our own and that conducted by other social scientists, tells us a lot about what memorable messages are, how they function, and how to get the most out of them. We believe that evidence-based guidance can improve people's lives, but figured most people who could benefit from insights into memorable messages aren't reading the densely written and jargon-filled research studies we publish in academic journals.

That's why we're here, and why we wrote this book. We want to make the concept of memorable messages, something both simple and powerful—the communication that sticks with us over time and impacts us in those profound ways—accessible to anyone who wants to learn about it. By trade, we are both social-behavioral scientists and educators, and we'll be wearing both of those hats throughout this book. But we also come to this book as ourselves—as people, women, friends, wives, and daughters sharing the messages we have received through the many roles that we occupy in our lives.

When the two of us joined the field of memorable message research, most of it focused on the types of messages that shape who we are and the people who share those socializing messages with us—our parents, teachers, or coworkers. Our own research on memorable messages about sex and sexual health offered a different sort of context. Many people grow up receiving messages about these subjects that are wildly inaccurate and unhelpful to them. As adults, many of those same folks acknowledge the inaccuracy: "This is what I was taught and it affected my behavior when I was younger, but now I know that's not true."

As a result of that research, we became interested in the idea of the space after one receives a memorable message—the trajectory of the message throughout our lifespan and how it continues to affect us (even if we later think it untrue). The communication process is not a one-way stream of talk where we receive a message and must be passively impacted by it. We remain active participants in the construction and reception of the messages we receive and how they ultimately affect us.

In this book, we make the argument that memorable messages are not just something that happens to us.

Communication doesn't just happen to us.

We are a part of the process, and we encourage you to be too. Memorable messages are an important part of the story of our lives—our experiences grounded and anchored by specific, impactful moments. But don't forget to follow the popular wisdom: Be your own storyteller.

1

Introducing Memorable Messages

"Healthy relationships are hard, but worth it."
"Honesty is the best policy."
"Pick your battles."
"Don't get old."
"Aging is a gift."
"Stand up for the little guy."
"Stay in your lane."
"Always say please and thank you."
"Treat everyone with respect."
"Never go to bed angry."
"Don't underestimate the power of first impressions."
"Raw garlic when you're sick."
"Count your blessings."
"Don't speak ill of the dead."
"Just try your best."
"You can't pour from an empty glass."
"Communication is key."

As teachers of communication, both of us have heard it more times than we can count.

The secret to a successful relationship? Communication.
The key to getting the most out of your job? Communication.
Healthy family dynamics? Communication.
Acing an interview? Managing conflict? Career growth?
Communication. Communication. Communication.

In many ways, research supports that sentiment. Communication processes account for relational and personal success in almost every important context—family,[1] friends,[2] romantic partners,[3] and even workplace,[4] healthcare,[5] and other public relationships. Even internal or intrapersonal communication—how we talk to ourselves—can profoundly influence us.[6] The messages that stay with us over time, like those above, impact us in many ways. But in order for communication to offer a solution to so many of our social and interpersonal challenges, we must take an active role in the process of creating, interpreting, and utilizing our memorable messages.

With that goal in mind, we have written this book as a space for readers to step actively and intentionally into that process. We want you to take ownership of the messages you share and receive. While we can't control the messages that other people send us, we have a lot of say in what we do with them. Before we introduce the more science-y details about what makes a message memorable and how those messages affect us over time, we want to start with a few of our own memorable messages.

Val: "In this family, we help people."

My mom repeated this message to me dozens of times throughout my childhood. I recall a hot summer day sometime during my teenage years, when I most certainly would have preferred to swim at the community pool or goof off in the passenger seat of my friend's car—celebrating those first steps of independence with a buddy's recent driver's license. Instead, you would find me covered in drying white paint in a sweltering apartment somewhere in Pittsburgh.

At that time, my grandfather owned and rented out a few properties. My mom often described him as a trusting man with a bleeding heart. As a result, tenants somewhat regularly trashed his properties. Rather than getting them into trouble for the damage, my grandfather, empathetic to their struggles, opted to help, so our family would clean up and repair the apartments between tenants, either for re-renting or selling—I don't recall which goal guided this particular instance. But I do remember the heat, the smell of the paint, my teenage grumbles, and, of course, my mom's steady refrain: "In this family, we help people."

Professionally and personally, my mother embodies the word "caregiver." She spent her entire career, from ages 19 to 70, working as a nurse. After raising two kids, she began caring for her aging parents shortly after I left home at 18. For my mom, "helping people" wasn't just a phrase meant to motivate a reluctant teenager—it was who she was. That's why the message resonated so deeply with me. It was genuine, rooted in authenticity, and reinforced by constant repetition, which is likely another reason I remember it to this day—because she said it all the time.

Angela: "Be careful..."

When I was around the age of nine, my mother, a dress designer by trade, faced the loss of her dress shop. The shop had been a dynamic part of our lives since I was a small child, and my mother's deep sadness over this loss felt palpable in our household. She'd worked her whole life to arrive at the possibility of having this dress shop. She sacrificed many long hours of sewing dresses, wedding gowns, and other outfits for the wealthy and everyday folk of greater Toledo, Ohio. When the shop closed, it was a dark time for her, and I recall her taking to bed—a fact that was never openly discussed in our family.

During this difficult time in my mother's life, one of her close friends paid a visit. I am not sure whether this happened in that moment of visitation or if she invited my mother to come with her to church, but I do remember the outcome. From what I recall, this became a time when my mother, who was genuinely a kind and lovely person with only occasional curse words, became a fortress of cautionary commentaries about "being careful."

Two "be carefuls" that remain cemented in my memory: "Be careful how you treat others, you might be attending angels unaware" and "Be careful how you treat people going up, you might meet them coming down." While my mother shared these sentiments prior to her new religious experience, they became more meaningful to her afterward. And, feeling her own authenticity in sharing them, I found her messages became more memorable to me.

The first "be careful," which resonated with me most, was intended to remind me and my siblings of being respectful and considerate to the strangers who crossed our paths. I'm sure this statement was simply meant to make the younger Angela aware that being brash or unkind to those who crossed my path was not acceptable; however, at such a young age, the idea that strangers could be spiritual beings sent to test our kindness deeply impacted me, fostering a sense of vigilance and curiosity about the mystical and spiritual world.

As I grew into a young adult, this message became more cemented in my mind and personality. I remember, while driving one day, pulling over to the curb to ask a stranger who looked stranded if they needed a ride. Before I knew it, they were in my car and I was taking them to their destination. When they got out of the car, I thought, "Well, that wasn't so smart, Angela." The stranger could have intended to harm me. Today and then, plenty of stories of young women alone volunteering to help a stranger end poorly. But then I quickly remembered the message from my mother—what if they were an angel? Call me naive, but this message from my dear mother still resonates with me to this day.

What Are Memorable Messages?

Do you remember the best advice you ever received? How about the worst? What words bring you comfort, especially in times of stress, difficulty, or pain? What did you need to hear, but never did? During the course of our lives, we receive more messages than we could ever realistically document in a text like this. Some of those messages stand out. They linger, maybe because we heard them repeated over and over. Or they last because we associate them with a person who means a lot to us. Maybe the moment you heard it carries significance. Sometimes they stay with us because they help us. Other times, these messages stick around because they hurt us. Often we repeat them ourselves, and often other people repeat them to us.

These messages that last over time are called *memorable messages*. Memorable messages are exactly what they sound like—a message that we remember. They're the messages that stick with us, the ones we recall amid the many thousands of other messages that occupy our communication throughout the course of our lives.[7]

We'll elaborate briefly here on those two components: memory and messages.

The concepts of memory and messages invoke both straightforward ideas and complex fields of social and behavioral science. Memory, in the context of memorable messages, refers simply to the fact that we recall these messages above and beyond other messages over our lifespan. Thinking back to your childhood, there are probably a handful of experiences that really stick with you, words of wisdom or comfort, maybe something that made you really happy or really sad. You had countless other communication experiences that never cemented into memory, but some did. The idea of memorable messages can help us explore why we remember those particular words, or that particular conversation, or that particular experience as opposed to all of the other words, conversations, or experiences that we don't remember.

Similarly, the idea of a "message" seems pretty simple on the surface. However, as communication books and classes often begin with, communication scientists actually have 126 different accepted definitions[8] of the term "communication." So what is a message? Or, said another way, what counts as communication as opposed to other forms of non-communication behavior? These questions form debates at the heart of communication science. We adopt the perspective that what makes a message *a message* is meaning.

The distinction between behavior that contains a message and behavior that doesn't lies in whether or not someone ultimately assigns meaning to that behavior. For example, while Val helped paint her grandfather's property, she probably pouted, the inflection of her words pointing to discontent or annoyance. The discontent and annoyance we associate with those nonverbal behaviors: meaning. Those ideas, embedded in words or actions by the sender or receiver, are the meaning we give a behavior, thereby making it a message.

Important to both the concept of meaning-making and to how we approach memorable messages throughout this book is the fact that meaning is not innate. A common axiom, a core principle, that we teach in our own communication classes, with some iteration in many communication textbooks,[9] is that "meanings are in people, not in words or behavior."

In a basic sense, this implies that the meanings of words or behavior are socially agreed upon—that's how language works, after all. But that agreement holds wide variation. For example, consider the word "dating." To one person, dating might mean going on dates. To another, dating might mean a committed relationship. Or consider the word "Christmas." To one person, that might evoke warm memories of a winter holiday spent with loved ones. To another, the word might mean a celebration that parts of the world engage in that means little to their own culture. To another, it might mean nostalgia over childhood memories. Or it might mean a time someone lost a loved one, a reminder of loneliness or tragedy. The many meanings we have for even just a singular word serve as a reminder that the meaning a message holds is deeply embedded within us, contextualized by our experiences, memories, and the relationship with the person who sent it to us.

We began this chapter by sharing some of our own memorable early family messages. These messages illustrate the basic principles of memorable messages that we'll introduce here. Specifically, they demonstrate both what makes a message memorable and how memorable messages can affect us.

Messages become memorable through three primary processes: *relationship*, *repetition*, and *utility*. Throughout this book, we elaborate on each of these principles and how we can leverage our understanding of them to make the most effective choices as communicators.

Relationship

Val's "In this family, we help people" and Angela's "Be careful" stand out, in part, because they came from our mothers—people we love and respect who played a significant role in raising us. Messages often become memorable because of the nature of the relationship between the sender and receiver of the message.[10] In many cases, the most influential messages come from parents or teachers, but especially mothers.[11]

As a teenager, Val might not have described her relationship with her mom in such glowing terms. Teen angst colored much of their interactions, and at the time, she didn't fully appreciate the values her mother tried to instill. As their relationship evolved, and as she grew up, she came to value those messages. Now Val sees her mother's messages as meaningful elements of her upbringing. Relationships can be tricky, and relationships with family, especially those that ebb and flow, can feel uncertain at times. Today, Val maintains a close relationship with her mother, and that relationship contributes to the memorability of the messages she received.

Similarly, Angela, as she will share in stories throughout the book, certainly did not always listen to her mother's messages when she first received them, but in hindsight, she considers her mother's many words of wisdom to be fundamental to how she lives her life as an adult. Angela's mother passed away many years ago, but she recalls the relationship with fondness and affection.

In our own research, as well as in decades of research conducted by others, mothers hold the title of author to many of our most memorable messages.[12,13] So it comes as no surprise that when thinking of the first message we both wanted to share in this book, words from our mothers sprang to mind. Many memorable messages in general come from people who are older, respected, of some kind of higher social (occupational or familial) status. But for many, moms hold a special place as conveyors of the kinds of messages, both good and bad, meant to stay with us over time.

Memorable messages can come from any source, but parents and teachers send many of our most memorable messages from childhood and adolescence. For both of us, our primary caregivers growing up were our mothers, so we will share a number of messages from our moms throughout this book. For others, those messages may come from their fathers, grandparents, stepparents, older siblings, or multiple people who played a big role in their childhood.

Our childhood memorable messages can affect us in both positive and negative ways. Importantly, while we both shared more positive examples from our relationships with our own mothers, certainly not everyone draws comfort or guidance from their maternal memorable messages. Strained, harmful, or otherwise unpleasant relationships can also contribute to a message's memorability. While mothers remain an important source of many of our collective memorable messages, our relationships with a whole variety of relational partners may lead us to remember the messages they send.

Repetition

Like many mothers and daughters, Val and her mom currently have a close relationship, but hostility and complaints better characterized their relationship during Val's teen years. Retrospectively, Val considers her mom a good mom, who tried to instill values like altruism and care for others and the world around us. But as many parents likely know, you have to say things more than once to a 16-year-old. Val's mom repeated that message of helping too many times for her to count, and while she can remember the details surrounding the enactment of that particular time, she could have easily recounted several others. Similarly, while Angela shared one instance of her remembering a "be careful," she could have shared many other times the words repeated aloud by her mother or in her own mind. You can likely think of your own messages that you heard over and over while growing up that stick with you to this day.

Messages often become memorable due to repetition.[14] We hear them over and over again. Sometimes message repetition occurs through the same source. In these examples, our moms repeated those messages many times. But other messages may become memorable because we hear them repeatedly through multiple sources, like friends or community members, or see stories reflected in television narratives or plastered on social media. For example, many of us recall some iteration of "treat others the way you want to be treated" because we heard it from multiple sources—parents, teachers, guidance counselors, even after-school specials or other media. This shared cultural message became memorable to many of us because we heard it from many sources, many times.

Utility

Messages are also memorable because we use them—we call upon them during times of need or incorporate them into our sense of self. Memorable messages persist because they prove useful to us in one way or another. For instance, helping people is central to how Val sees her family identity—what defines her family and her role within it. Angela's "be careful" advice comes to mind during moments of decision-making, reminding her to consider her actions (even when they're somewhat risky). Messages may also prove useful if they contribute to our identity. We will talk about this more as an outcome rather than a feature of memorability, but when a message becomes incorporated into how we see ourselves, we are also more likely to remember them.

The utility of a message—its practical value in our lives—contributes to its staying power. When messages resonate with our experiences or help us navigate difficult situations, they become integrated into how we see ourselves and the world around us.

Utility is an important idea when thinking about memorable messages, especially those that may prove less benign and altruistic than the ones in our opening stories. A lot of the messages we hear, and many we'll explore throughout this book, are *not* useful. When we encounter experiences in our lives where we would call upon those messages, sometimes they don't help us or point us in the right direction. Or maybe we just don't agree with them anymore.

The stories we shared in this chapter also illustrate how memorable messages affect us in three key ways: relationships, identity, and behavior. We'll explore these concepts in more depth throughout the book, looking at how the messages we receive shape who we are and the choices we make. Here, we want to introduce what we'll call the three basic outcomes of memorable messages, or the three primary ways that these messages affect us over time.

Relationships

The relationship aspect of memorable messages works both ways. Sometimes we remember these messages because of the significance of our relationship with the person who delivered them, but those messages can also shape and influence our relationships. This occurs in both positive and negative ways, but we want to begin with some positive ones.

The messages we remember from childhood are often

memorable because we had or have close relationships with the people who shared them. The content and quality of those messages also contribute to the strength of those relationships—or sometimes explain the strain on those relationships.[15] For example, when Val reflects on the important messages her mother shared, she easily recalls those that validated, encouraged, and challenged her to do good in the world. This particular message fits into a category that nurtures and sustains a more fulfilling relationship with her mom. Alternatively, folks who recall more harmful, negative, or dismissive messages may notice that those interactions impacted the quality of the relationship within which they occurred. Someone who recalls messages that made them feel bad or small from a parent likely does not have the best relationship with that parent in adulthood.

Memorable messages in many ways reflect the relationships we have with the people from whom we received those messages. The messages we remember can characterize our relationships as loving, safe, and warm, or hostile, hurtful, and cold. In addition to impacting how we see others, memorable messages can influence how we see ourselves.

Identity

One of the ways we learn who we are, who we should be, how to act in the many situations we encounter in life, and how we fit into our family and the world around us is through memorable messages. These messages shape our identities and self-concepts. Both of our opening examples identified key characteristics of our family identities: helpfulness and kindness. In Val's case, the message directly articulated her family's values. Later in the book, Angela will share several examples of memorable messages that spoke to her own family's identity.

As we mentioned, helping others is central to how Val sees her role in the family. As such, she has internalized this message, and by endorsing its content, it has become part of her own identity and self-concept. It also reflects her broader family identity. While we were writing this book, Val's grandfather, who lived to 98, passed away. At his funeral, the priest shared stories about how helpful and altruistic he was. Pap, as the family called him, would help anyone who needed it, day or night. Throughout her childhood, Val remembers seeing him on her parents' porch, sometimes late into the night. He was always fixing something for someone. At the funeral, as speakers shared stories about his innate helpfulness, Val noticed her mom and aunts exchanging knowing looks, reaffirming this core element of their family identity. When Val's mom repeated the message, "In this family, we help people," she was actively socializing Val into seeing her family the same way she did—as helpful.

The emotional reactions we experience and hold onto surrounding memorable messages often revolve around concepts of self and identity. These messages ultimately shape how we see ourselves and others, and they can trigger both positive and negative emotional responses. Because Val accepted helping people as a part of her family identity, it also became a standard by which she compared her behavior.

Behavior

At the end of Angela's opening "be careful" story, she notes that she used her mother's memorable message to reflect on a risky but kind choice she made to give a stranger a ride. This offers an example of what social scientists call *behavioral self-assessment*. Behavioral self-assessment, or looking back on what we do in day-to-day life and considering if it embodies how we see ourselves (or sometimes how we *want* to see ourselves), is another outcome of our memorable messages.

For instance, we might make a choice that reflects the part of our identity we see as helpful by actively choosing to assist someone we perceive as being in need. Or we might make a choice where we don't. Instead of driving a friend to the airport, maybe we make an excuse for why we're busy that day. If we choose that course of action, our process of reflecting on that choice and how it ultimately makes us feel about ourselves (probably kind of bad) is in part because of the way messages like Val's "in this family, we help people" or Angela's "be careful" weigh on our self-concept and influence how we assess our own behavior.

Taking actions that live up to that standard likely make us feel better about ourselves, and taking actions that don't can make us feel worse. For example, though giving a stranger a ride might seem risky or unsafe, the memorable message Angela recalled made her feel better about the decision because it aligned with the values her mother instilled. Her actions lived up to the standard of kindness her memorable messages embedded.

Research also shows that we attribute memorable messages to influencing our actual behavior. In other words, we use memorable messages both to make sense of or explain the choices we've already made, and to directly shape future choices. For example, one research study found that memorable messages from healthcare providers about diet and exercise resulted in people reporting that they ate healthier foods and exercised more.[16] In another study, 70 percent of college students reported changing their behavior when recalling memorable messages aimed at helping them manage college life.[17] Memorable messages can and do directly influence the choices we make and the behaviors we enact.

Whenever we really think about our actions (and let's be honest, we don't always), and we face a choice about whether or not to help someone, our early messages often come to mind. For the two of us, the messages we've received, especially from our moms, influence our behavior. We all have messages like that—ones that make us stop, reflect, and explain the choices we make. Memorable messages are powerful because they shape not only how we think and feel about our actions, but sometimes the actions themselves.

"Don't have sex until you're married."
"Always call me if you need a ride home."
"If you need help, you can always ask me."

Form and Function

Collectively, these elements of memorability and outcome we have introduced so far help shape a function of memorable messages that social scientists call *anticipatory socialization*, which is a very academic way of describing the messages and experiences that tell us what to expect in the future, and what to do, choose, or how to behave in those future instances. In other words, anticipatory socialization describes the process of learning what to do when something happens someday.

Take, for example, "Always call me if you need a ride home," a common message a parent might send to a teenager or adolescent embarking on more independent decision-making. Simply, that message instructs their child that if they face a situation where they might need help, they can call their parents. This is an example of anticipatory socialization, sharing a message that helps someone anticipate a future need or choice, and directs them about what to do in that situation.

Early research suggested that most memorable messages follow a pretty similar form as *prescriptive messages,*[18] messages that advise people about what to do in the future, like the examples shared above. Although a considerable amount of research has demonstrated that memorable messages take a variety of linguistic forms, and often don't sound directly like advice at all,[19] many messages still follow that prescriptive formula—telling people what to do in different situations. While not all messages sound like advice or direction, many of those same messages still serve the purpose of anticipatory socialization.[20]

So far, we've briefly introduced what memorable messages do. Now, we will introduce what they look and sound like. Memorable messages can be direct, indirect, or ambient, or they can be evident by their omission. Let's break those different message types down a little.

Direct messages, like those described so far in this chapter, include advice, or someone telling you what to do, or other verbally delivered messages. Our opening stories provide examples. But messages can also be *indirect*—for instance, someone sharing a story that we take a particular message from, or sharing a message to someone else in your presence. For example, perhaps a parent instructs your sibling to be extra careful when driving home at night. Even if you were not the direct recipient of that message—it wasn't intended for you—you might have internalized and remembered "be extra careful when driving at night." Alternatively, perhaps the parent tells you a story about a risky choice they made growing up. While never explicitly uttering the lesson of the story, you may take the message "think twice about your choices." Even though the parent never directly said those words, remembering the lesson or theme can still form a memorable message. Messages are about meaning. The exact words are much less significant than the meaning we ultimately take away from a message. Thus, many memorable messages occur through indirect means.

Ambient messages also become memorable. These describe memorable personal experiences.[21] For example, if your parents fought a lot, you might internalize ambient messages from the experience of hearing their conflict, even if they did not deliver a specific verbal message to you or in your presence.

Alternatively, sometimes we encounter circumstances in life when we need to hear something from someone close to us. When navigating major transitions, first relationships, graduations, weddings, new jobs, major losses, and grief, we expect the people closest to us to leave us with messages we will remember. When that doesn't happen, we often remember that too—the absence of a message we needed to hear. Or sometimes what they say sticks with us, but in ways that we find less helpful or useful. The *omission of needed meaning* also remains memorable to us over time.

All of these messages, regardless of the form they take, can serve the function of socializing us, telling us what to expect in the future, or how we ought to behave in the present.

Throughout this book, we'll dive into the ways that our own memorable messages prepare us (or sometimes fail to prepare us) for the lives that we live and the circumstances that we ultimately encounter. When messages prepare us well for our lived experiences, they can encourage self-acceptance, self-esteem, hope, and resilience. When messages fail to lay the groundwork for the world we eventually confront, we can feel unprepared or uncertain. Worse, some messages make us feel hurt, rejected, or isolated.

"No matter what, we'll always love you."
"You can do it!"
"Always believe in yourself and trust your gut."

Many of the messages we receive bring us comfort or help us navigate challenging life transitions. For instance, students beginning high school or college may recall memorable messages that help them consider what to do in new academic environments. Young people embarking on marriage may recall parental relationship messages that help shape their worldview about relationships, or advise them on how to proceed during early marital conflict.[22] People starting a new job may rely on the wisdom of friends and parents who have provided them messages that instruct their behavior in a new organization, or the messages from more senior coworkers who orient them to the new workplace.[23] Students faced with decisions about how to prioritize their time between homework and sporting activities or what kinds of questions to bring to their advisors, or a young married person considering how to approach their new spouse about differing perspectives on finances, all may draw on these memorable messages to guide them. When we're anxious, stressed, or grieving, we might find comfort in memorable messages from parents, peers, and elders who shared the right words to get through it.

"You're not smart enough for that."
"Keep your feelings to yourself."
"Suck it up."

But we also encounter situations and experiences in life for which we're not prepared. Young people often stumble through their early relational and sexual encounters with little realistic guidance that meets the expectations of their lived experiences. Students encounter a different academic landscape than the one their parents navigated. Entry-level workers often face different standards and expectations than their more senior colleagues. Sometimes advice doesn't land, or those important conversations never took place at all. Worse, sometimes messages sent undermine an individual's sense of self-confidence, make them feel incapable, or lead to them feeling hurt or dismissed.

Who are we and who is this book for?

The content of this book is personal, and we ask our readers to engage with your own personal stories throughout this text. We want to take a second to introduce ourselves. At the time of writing this book, both of us worked as communication professors for state universities (on opposite sides of the country, Val in Maine and Angela in California). In addition to teaching, we are social and behavioral scientists. Between the two of us, we have 74 peer-reviewed publications, many of them about memorable messages. We coedited the book *Communicating Intimate Health*, which focused on the ways that memorable messages inform gendered and intimate health and healthcare experiences. We have also written the "Theory of Memorable Messages" and edited a special volume of the peer-reviewed journal *LGBTQ+Family* on memorable messages.

Beyond that, Val currently lives with her spouse (Sam), two chunky cats (Benz and Loki), and a little dog (Deborah) who likes to wear silly sweaters. She grew up in a middle-class family, raised in a pretty non-religious environment in Pittsburgh by parents who were raised Catholic (mother) and Jewish (father), but neither still practiced by the time she came into the world. She has a brother and remains close with her large extended family. She likes to run, play video games, hike (very casually), make earrings and other crafts, and spend time with people she cares about.

Angela is a self-proclaimed transient, having lived in six different states over the course of 30 years. She and her partner have lived in Vermont, Ohio, Kentucky, New Mexico, Massachusetts, and now California. Because of this, she prides herself on being a minimalist, which is simply a result of all the moves they have been through. She's the youngest of five siblings. She loves watercolor painting, and while new to tennis has become quite good at playing.

We believe memorable messages are a part of life that many people understand intuitively and want to explore further. To that end, we bring our professional and personal selves to this book. Our expertise in memorable messages is the primary driving force behind choosing to write this, but we also come to the study of memorable messages through the lens of our lived experiences. While the two of us, by trade, are social/behavioral scientists and draw from both social and behavioral research, which has spent the last 40 years publishing dozens of research studies on the concept of memorable messages, and our own extensive theorizing on the topic, we do not intend this as a strictly academic book. We have written extensively about memorable messages for other social scientists and for students of communication and psychology. While we invite that audience to enjoy this as well, this book is meant for everyone. No prior knowledge on this subject necessary.

In addition to sharing what the research says about memorable messages, we draw heavily from our own experiences both as behavioral researchers and as people who have made and received our own memorable messages throughout our lives. We'll also share many examples of memorable messages that our participants have shared with us over the years through our research studies. You'll notice that we shift perspective in writing throughout this book. As our stories are personal to us, we take a more personal tone when sharing our own messages and past experiences. We encourage you to do the same.

What Are Your Memorable Messages?

In the following chapters, we'll talk through how memorable messages function in more detail, how to get the most out of meaningful and valuable memorable messages, and elaborate on what to do when memorable messages ultimately don't serve us anymore. We also invite the reader to consider your own memorable messages throughout this book. What are they? Who shared them with you? What words would you use to describe how they make you feel? How do you feel about the person who sent them? Are these messages valuable, constructive, or insightful? Alternatively, are they harmful, invalidating, or mean? Maybe they are relatively neutral, but just didn't help in the situation they meant to help in. Or maybe they were immensely helpful.

If you aren't sure where to begin, try the beginning. Think about your childhood or adolescence. What was a memorable message someone shared with you during that time period? While you are welcome to answer our prompts here and throughout this book only in your head, we do encourage you to write your answers down. We're big believers in the power of journaling, because committing words to paper is one way to take ownership of your communication journey. So take a minute or a few minutes and write down a memorable message you recall from your childhood. If you are reading this as an ebook, we encourage you to dedicate a small journal or notepad to the process. If you are reading a physical copy, feel free to use the book itself to address these prompts.

Reread or repeat the message aloud to yourself. Consider:

- Why do you think that you remember this message?
- How often did you hear this message?
- What were the circumstances surrounding the reception of this message?
- Who sent it to you? How did you feel about them when they sent it to you?
- How do you feel about them now?
- How did this message make you feel when you heard it?
- How does it make you feel now?
- Do you think the message was useful to you?

Take some space here to reflect on those questions.

Now, and any time we invite you to participate in this book with your own experiences, feel empowered to write as little or as much as you want. If you can't remember some element of your past, that's okay. When we shared our own memories at the beginning of this chapter, the stories we documented here may not reflect every detail of the actual experiences they depicted. These are our memories from exchanges that we experienced decades ago. Memory is fallible and imperfect, but it's a part of us. What you remember matters, even if it's not accurate or complete. Learning from our memorable messages means not getting too hung up on those details right now. For now, encourage yourself to let the emotional response to the memory guide your answers.

To start, we'll dig a little deeper into the idea of message repetition. Specifically, we'll consider why so many of us share the same memorable messages. We'll share examples of common memorable messages in a variety of contexts, and invite you to consider where your own memorable messages join or deviate from the masses.

Content Warnings

Before proceeding, we wanted to take a brief moment to list some of the subjects we talk about. Throughout this book, we do dive into sensitive topics and conversations that people recall. Some of these topics include body size, diet and exercise, disordered eating behaviors, mental health, sexual identity, parental relationships, domestic violence, racism, and healthcare interactions.

2

Repetition

Why do so many of us share the same memorable messages?

"You catch more flies with honey than vinegar."
"Hard work pays off."
"Treat others the way you want to be treated."
"Work smarter, not harder."
"Find the time for what matters."

Parents, teachers, media and religious leaders, and even peers, partners and friends repeat messages to us over and over again. A significant reason for why memorable messages stick with us over time is repetition. In general, memories often form through repetition. For memorable messages, repetition occurs in two primary ways. Sometimes the same person repeats messages to us; for instance, a parent repeatedly telling their child to look both ways before crossing the street. Other times, multiple sources repeat the same messages, usually emphasizing cultural values. For example, most people who grew up in the U.S. received messages about the value of hard work. These messages likely came from family, teachers, community leaders, and popular media.

In this chapter, we'll discuss how message repetition functions as part of memory formation, what it looks like when messages get repeated by the same source, and what happens when we hear messages from multiple sources. We'll discuss why so many of us share so many similar memorable messages and how message repetition perpetuates larger cultural values and narratives.

To begin, let's consider some of your own memorable messages. Think about some of the messages that you've heard pretty often throughout your life. These repeated messages don't need to be word-for-word the same if repeated by different sources, but should capture the spirit or intention of the message. For instance, we might recall a message about work ethic from a parent ("Hard work pays off"), from teachers ("Always try your best"), and from popular culture through general depictions in stories that reward hard work or punish depictions of laziness. We can describe this as roughly the same message, even if it sounds a little different when repeated by different sources.

Or you might have heard the same message that one person told you over and over, like a parent repeating that they love you. Consider:

- What are some messages you received many times?
- How often do you think you heard those messages?
- Did you hear them from one source, or multiple sources?
- What does each message mean to you?
- Why do you think you heard these messages as often as you did?

Remember, messages are about meaning. The exact word-for-word message matters less here than the meaning you took from those messages.

One Message, One Message Source

In the last chapter, Val shared a story, noting that her mother repeated a family memorable message, *"In this family, we help people,"* frequently throughout her childhood and adolescence. The story she shared recalls one meaningful instance among many, many others. Val's mom shared the message at least dozens of times when she was growing up, probably intentionally, to share a desired family identity and instill a moral value in her child. Parents share the same message repeatedly to pass along desired values to their children. To demonstrate, consider an example of Angela's message repetition:

"Neglect Not the Gift Within You."

An artifact I hold dear is a heart-shaped note that my mother gave me early in my teenage life. On it she had written simply, "neglect not the gift within you," its intent amplified by the fact that she'd put it on a piece of paper cut into the shape of a heart. Even though she passed away many years ago—1998—I've kept this cherished note tucked away in one of my favorite scrapbooks. My mother told me time and time again: "neglect not the gift within you," especially when I was frustrated by her teaching me to sew my first garment and many thereafter, or when I took voice and piano lessons. I love that these words helped me push the boundaries of what I didn't always feel comfortable doing.

I think because my mother was a multi-talented person who had numerous interests and aspirations, she infused the same aspirations in her children, her grandchildren, and other family members to unpack our "gifts." Many of my mother's gifts came to fruition. She was a talented seamstress; her father taught her to sew when she was young. As an adult, she was the first woman to own a Black business in a very segregated Sylvania, Ohio, community—her talent as a dressmaker was highly revered. When her shop closed, she decided to go back to school to earn a degree in education. In midlife, she became an elementary school teacher in Toledo and later took a position as a principal at a middle school. As her passion for education and teaching children from underserved communities grew, she became interested in returning to school to get her PhD in education when she was in her late 60s. Even before getting her college degrees, she committed many Friday evenings to convening all the children from our neighborhood to attend her Bible clubs. Her message to "neglect not the gift" embodied everything she believed in and held dear. As an adult, I've always been appreciative that my mother taught me to be daring, trust my gut, and not be afraid of the difficult things that push against my life. This one message and one message source—my mom—became a central memorable message in my life pursuits that she repeated to us many times and that I believed because she embraced it herself.

Individuals repeat the same message, sometimes strategically, to reinforce it. In a basic sense, repetition is just a part of how our memories work. Repetition, as well as the order of repeated experiences, work together in building memories.[1] As teachers and parents tend to intuitively know, repeating information helps us learn. In fact, repetition and learning are so interconnected that good teachers build repetition into their lesson plans. Parents repeat messages meant to instill ideals or values in their children over and over again so that their children learn what the message meant to teach. "Treat other people the way you want to be treated," "say please and thank you," and "look both ways before crossing the street" will be repeated many times by parents and teachers until they feel the message recipients have learned the desired lessons.

Neuroscience and the psychology of memory are two significant fields of study in which stating *repetition impacts memory formation* would seem like a massive understatement. The relationship between repetition and memory forms entire scientific agendas, with research studies exploring our complex cognitive machinery that takes information from the world around us and turns it into what an individual "knows." Repetition helps us store long-term memories and impacts the kinds of memory-related judgments that we're likely to make.[2]

Unsurprisingly, then, the more we hear a particular message, the more likely that message is to become memorable to us. Individuals with whom we have the opportunity for many interactions over time, like parents, grandparents, or teachers, form many of our memorable message sources, especially from childhood.[3] In part, they become our memorable message sources because they simply have the most opportunities to repeat messages to us, again and again.

Interpersonal repetition also helps families and individuals establish the values that define their family system and relationship culture. Parents repeat many messages to children to prepare and socialize them for the world, but they also repeat messages to their children to tell them who they ought to be and what they should value. Romantic partners may repeat the same messages to characterize their relationship culture, such as "In this relationship, we tell each other everything." Repeating messages to one's partner, child, sibling, or friend can help cement the message into memory and reinforce the value as characteristic of that relationship.

But we don't just exist in one place, and our family alone does not socialize us. Each of us also exists as a part of a larger culture that inundates us with many messages. Even many messages repeated by the same message source have a tendency to reflect larger cultural values. For example, take messages about honesty. In the U.S., many messages encourage children to see honesty as a core value.

For example, they may hear "lying is bad" or "honesty is always the best policy" repeatedly from their parents. But they likely also hear that message from their teachers and see it reflected in stories in the media. As a result, a lot of us might report memorable messages that sound kind of familiar. Maybe the wording is a little different, or maybe the circumstances surrounding the receipt of that message vary, but the spirit of the message can sound awfully similar.

One Message, Multiple Message Sources

"You might not feel that way in a few years."
"Sex is for men."
"You don't owe anyone sex."

A lot of our own research focuses on memorable messages in the context of gendered health, messages younger women receive about their bodies, and sexuality more broadly. The examples shared before this paragraph in fact come from a specific study we did on memorable messages that LGBTQ women recall.[4] Across multiple research studies, we have formally collected hundreds of memorable messages on those subjects and heard many more in presenting and speaking about our research. Although the messages we find might not be worded exactly the same, a couple of shared themes occur again and again across populations and contexts. That's because they reflect larger cultural ideas. These messages can come from our family system, which might seek to establish a unique family identity or one that endorses shared values with their community, religion, or other culture. Alternatively, these repeated cultural messages may come from the media, peers, teachers, or others. These messages repeat the cultural values of the time. To illustrate, Val describes the memorable messages that impacted her coming-out experience.

"Coming Out Changes Your Relationships."

Despite occupying a role as a pretty publicly out lesbian, who has a reputation as a sexual relationship researcher, who teaches classes on sex, sexuality, and diverse relationships, and who is most certainly not shy when it comes to talking about sex, I almost never talk about my own coming out, in part because the popular depiction of coming out as a onetime dramatic event, as queer people are well aware, is pretty unrealistic. For instance, as I write this story, I'm wrapping up my first week of teaching for a new school year. I have 137 students this semester, and that means I just came out to 137 new people (I always share a picture of me and my spouse during my self-introduction). Queer people negotiate coming out constantly, with every new interaction. For those like my spouse, whom I would call more visibly queer, people probably make assumptions about their sexuality when they see them. But for folks like me, aside from some bright lipstick, a tiny tattoo of rainbow dots on my arm, and a few colored streaks only visible if I pull my long hair up, my femininity can make my queerness invisible unless I choose to tell people. I almost always do. I'm married, and my relationship is an important part of my life, and I teach and write about identity, so sharing my own identity feels authentic and important. But despite coming out almost daily in my professional life, I don't actually talk about the process very often.

Another reason I may avoid sharing my coming-out experiences: I have been extraordinarily lucky that they have largely been uneventful. In my professional life, the only real consequence is the occasional homophobic student evaluation (the vast majority of students I've encountered either couldn't care less about my sexuality, or indicate excitement at having a gay professor, so I would emphasize that the homophobic evaluations are a very small minority in my own experience, but I know that's not true for many others). In my personal network, the only negative responses I have received about my identity came from distant connections—a homophobic great-uncle who made a crappy comment once to my mom, or an off-handed comment by an ex-boyfriend (I did date guys once upon a time) that reflected his insecurity. But for my friends and close family, pretty much everyone important I have ever come out to has been kind and supportive, and I've never lost or had a relationship damaged as a result. As both a queer person and a queer researcher, I would say, both anecdotally and empirically, that having had neither serious personal or professional consequences to sharing my identity are uncommon and extremely privileged perspectives from which to talk about coming out. But my own coming-out experiences, uneventful as they might have ultimately been in retrospect, reflect the many ways that cultural messages, repeated to us over and over again, result in shared memorable messages.

Of the important, lasting personal relationships I held in my life during the years I was realizing and labeling my sexuality—my later teen years and even into my early 20s—my parents were the last people I told. Given the praise I have shared already for my mother, that might sound surprising. I grew up in a liberal household, my parents never said a single disparaging statement about queer folks in my hearing, they were kind and welcoming to my gay friends when I was younger. Neither parent offered any indication that they would not react well to the news. Still, by the time basically every other member of my family and all of my friends knew my identity, I had not yet told my parents.

As my mother still occasionally complains about, it ended up being years after my 15-year-old-self first nervously admitted to a friend that I thought I liked girls before I anxiously wrote an email to my parents, coming out. Both of them responded as would be expected for anyone who knew them. They tried to acknowledge it was a moment for me, but ultimately it didn't change much. My mom called me and told me she loved me. My dad wrote me a sweet email in response. In my heart, I knew that was how they would react before I clicked send. I knew my parents. Had they reacted negatively, that would have been a confusing shift in character from the people who raised me.

But I was still terrified to tell them, and that anxiety led to years of holding my brother, and cousins, and even an aunt, who I mentioned a girlfriend to more than a year before I ultimately told my own mother, to secrecy. You may be asking yourself: "Why did she put herself through that if she knew deep down her parents would be cool about it?" The answer isn't just because I was young and uncertain, although I was. It's because even though I knew my parents as people, I also thought of them as "parents." In a prototypical sense, the idea of "parents" as a category for people within cultural coming-out narratives has a particular reputation for types of reaction.

When I was in high school, a friend's mom passed away. I recall my friend sharing that on her deathbed, she told him she didn't accept the choice he had made to be gay. Throughout my late teens and early 20s, I heard so many stories from queer friends of parents bringing the priest to their house when they came out. I heard stories of friends who were kicked out of their home, rejected from their family, or financially cut off prematurely. Even for friends whose parents might not have cut them off completely, the news changed their relationship, chilled a previously warm home, or left them feeling that at the end of the day, their parents wished they were straight. Stories of coming-out trauma and drama filled my teens and young adulthood.

Personal anecdotes confirmed fears reflected in movies and television shows. Optimistically, I see a lot more diverse representations of queerness and coming out in the media today, but in the early 2000s, a younger Val saw few queer folks on television, and watched coming-out stories that did exist rarely presenting the possibility of continuing a relationship as it was. A character's queerness, even in the extremely rare stories where it was accepted, always changed the dynamics, usually for the worse.

Family systems have a lot of potential to insulate us against harmful cultural messages. Because of how my parents raised me, when I realized I was gay, I never felt shame about that. I wasn't embarrassed or upset to discover that part of myself. But family systems rarely prepare us for all of the cultural messages we'll encounter. As far as I know, my parents never suspected their traditionally feminine teenage daughter, who was grounded on more than one occasion for sneaking boys into the house when her parents weren't home, as being anything other than heterosexual, so they never felt the need to counter messages related to coming out. But we knew gay people, so they did counter messages about homophobia and heterosexism. So I rejected the messages I received from our larger culture that told me being gay was wrong, but I accepted the messages that telling your family you were gay would change your relationships. And I was afraid to change those relationships.

Ultimately, those fears induced by cultural and interpersonal memorable messages about what coming out would do to those relationships never came to light. My parents reacted fine, and our relationships, if anything, improved since I was no longer keeping an unnecessary secret from them. In the near decade-and-a-half since, my early fears about coming out have never really been realized. While I'm not alone in having lucked into a supportive network at an early age, and while I'm pleased to see more diverse representations of coming out in the media these days, the messages that fueled my adolescent and young adult fears didn't come from nowhere. A lot of queer people do lose or alter their family relationships, facing rejection or even violence in coming out. My parents never delivered a memorable message to me that suggested coming out would be bad, but I received so many other messages telling me that it would *be bad that I was still paralyzed by that anxiety for years.*

Lastly, I never really like talking about coming out because it recalls a time before I wrote about period sex and gave lectures on feminist erotica, when I wasn't an open book about my own identity. In my defense, few are open books in their teens or early 20s. We're still learning who we are, and most of us aren't ready to really communicate it. But while we're figuring it out, we are also being told who we should be and how people will react to it by a constant stream of cultural memorable messages.

Cultural Narrative Repetition

Narrative repetition,[5] as researchers call it, occurs when we repeat stories, sometimes within other stories, over time. Memorable messages can take many forms, and for some of us, they occur in the form of stories rather than short messages. Coming-out stories can form one kind of narrative repetition, resulting in memorable messages shared across many times, peoples, and places. When asking LGBTQ+ individuals across multiple research studies what coming out looks like, they often describe similar basic themes.[6,7] The reason these individuals, who come from a variety of backgrounds, describe the same basic experiences, even if their own experience differed, is because they draw from the same set of repeated stories shared by friends and the same media through books, TV shows, movies, and the culture at large.

Of course, coming-out messages only offer one of many repeated cultural narratives that form core expectations and understandings of life for so many of us. Memorable message research typically positions these acts of communication as most effective and memorable when delivered interpersonally. This means that we often find messages more memorable and more impactful if someone tells us the message directly (rather than hearing about it secondhand or watching it on TV), and usually even more so if it's someone we know and care about. We'll get into the role of message sender relationships in the next chapter, but messages delivered via mass media are not unimportant. Even general experiences—those ambient or indirect messages, words said in our company but not directed at us, flyers, blogs, reels, and anything else—can form a memorable message, especially when they are repeated and reinforced. In the modern media landscape, where young people's social world is heavily curated through a screen, the messages shared in many forms and modalities matter more than ever.

"If you keep letting her eat, she's going to get fat."
"If you can pinch an inch."
"Your body is your temple."

For another example, let's consider another thread of memorable message research that looks at "body" messages. These are what they sound like—memorable messages that tell people how to feel about their bodies, diet and exercise, body image satisfaction, and so on. For example, a frequent message from one of Val's research studies, "It's better to be depressed skinny than happy fat,"[8] echoes a common (and harmful) cultural message that people receive about body image satisfaction. People report hearing that kind of message not just from one individual in their life, but from many—ranging from direct statements ("You'll be happier if you lose weight") to messages taken from observing other people's behavior (such as children hearing adults discuss dieting or describing dissatisfaction with their own bodies).

Unsurprisingly, the bulk of these messages emphasize a cultural value of thinness, equating health with being small, and suggesting the core of one's value lies in how others view their body. Obviously, these messages can be harmful, especially to populations at increased risk for disordered eating.

Sometimes these messages come from an interpersonal source and are delivered only to the message recipient in the form of a conversation. Teenagers and college students report messages from parents, coaches, and peers that emphasize those values. But those messages are also endorsed and repeated across the media. Visual depictions of desired and valuable people that all look kind of the same, discussions of health and wellness that surround dietary behavior, and cultural narratives that position thinness as valued and good[9] all reinforce those interpersonal messages,[10] lending what *feels* like truth to them. When you hear the same thing from enough people, it seems more and more legitimate, meaning we're more likely to buy it and it's more likely to influence our behavior and future conversations.

Culturally informed messages repeat over time as well—making their way through the generations. For a different example, take an informal chat that Angela had with a student about how her own family messages, filtered through cultural and religious traditions, impacted her experiences:

For context, I teach at a Hispanic serving institution, which means my classrooms have a large representation of Hispanic and Latina/o/e students. After class one day, a student and I were walking in the same direction to a common parking structure on campus. As we walked, we began chatting about her academic experiences as a student at the university. During this conversation, we began talking about me and my work. Shyly, she admitted that she had looked me up on Google and had found a few of my articles on sexual health really fascinating. I asked, "which ones?"

She responded, "Well, the one you wrote about menstruation was super interesting." I asked her to explain why she found it interesting. In response, she continued, "well.... I loved swimming when I was young but when I started my period I had to stop."

With some initial confusion, I asked, "Why?"

"Well, my mother said that swimming meant I had to use tampons and I wasn't allowed to wear them because they would derail my purity—take away my virginity. We never talked about how but I knew this was a taboo product and topic," she said.

I contemplated how to respond. Realizing my face betrayed disconcertment, I took a deep breath and asked, "Where did your mother hear that information?"

She said matter-of-factly, "That's what her mother told her."

"Ah, I see," I said, of course quickly adding, "So you know that's not true, right?"

"Well, now I do, but this sort of conversation—telling your daughters this—is typical in my community. My sisters hear the same information—sometimes we're told this makes us dirty or loose ... wearing a tampon," she lamented.

We kept chatting on our walk to the parking lot. Eventually she shared, "Now, when I want to go swimming, I put in a tampon and go." It turned out that she had actually taken a swimming course last semester. But she chose not to share this information with her mother. Despite knowing her memorable message from her mother was untrue, she knew the idea was something her mother still held as truth. We got to our cars before I was able to ask more about why she hadn't talked with her mother or grandmother, if she'd shared more accurate information with her younger sibling or talked with her Latina girlfriends, or how she negotiated spaces where misinformation, messages that were not accurate, impacted her and her community.

In this instance, Angela's student shared a memorable message she attributed to her and her mother's shared cultural identities as Latina. Her student also believed these ideas stemmed from religious messages that her mother, and her grandmother before that, grew up hearing. This student shared that her memorable message impacted her behavior directly when she was younger—avoiding wearing a tampon and engaging in an activity, swimming, that she enjoyed. Now, the student rejects the validity of the message, returning to swimming and wearing tampons when necessary, but it still impacts her behavior in a different way. She chooses not to share certain information with her mother because she knows her mother does believe that. These messages circulate through generations due to repetition. Hearing them again and again, they can feel like the truth, even if there is no scientific basis to them.

Messages we hear repeated over and over aren't always negative. We may also share memorable messages about the importance of love, family, or kindness. Cultural values promoted through these repeated narratives can form a basis for many of the memorable messages we ultimately end up hearing and recalling. While we may belong to some shared cultures, we also probably deviate—belonging to many cultures that vary by income, education, racial ethnic group, religion, language culture, sexuality, region, and even some interests.

Different cultural groups share different messages that reflect the values associated with those cultures.

Repetition can also serve to emphasize importance. Large-scale, public events can form lasting message memories as well. Scientists call these flashbulb memories, which are associated with learning about some kind of significant public event.[11] For example, most of us can recall where we were when we first heard about the terrorist attacks of September 11, 2001. The detail with which we can describe learning about these circumstances, even if we were not directly impacted in any way, emphasizes the role of cultural value in memory formation. Significant shared social experiences like those form the basis of these often very detailed memories and provide important others in our lives with opportunities to deliver more messages.

But for memorable messages, the circumstances surrounding message receipt—*where were you, what was happening, how old were you*—are often less important than *how often* you heard the message, *from whom* you heard it, and how it *made you feel*. Still, for memories considered culturally important, like major historical events, those details come easier for most of us.

Culture, a complicated concept, describes the stuff going on around us outside of our closer relational bubbles. But culture also affects those relationships. Family messages can reflect larger cultural values and impact our cultural socialization.[12] That is, these messages from our family help tell us what it means to be a member of a particular culture. This is another reason that people, especially people raised in similar cultures, share similar family messages even when raised in different families. For an example, take Angela's story about a common type of message many of us received around work ethic:

"Don't put off until tomorrow what you could do today."

A few messages in my household embodied having a strong work ethic and fortitude like "the early bird catches the worm" or, the most memorable because we heard it so frequently as young kids, "don't put off until tomorrow what you could do today." In a household with four sisters, my older brother often got saddled with certain chores.

Every Saturday morning before we could leave the house, go hang with friends, or go out to play, we heard "don't put off until tomorrow what you could do today," which meant it was time to clean the house for the upcoming week.

I cannot remember exactly how many times I heard "don't put off...." My siblings and I heard it so often that when my mother spoke the first three words, we all in harmony finished her sentence "until tomorrow what you could do today." For my brother, I believe there was so much more tied to this statement. He was vigilant with his life aspirations. He knew very early that he wanted to attend a Historically Black University and I believe deep down his diligence in "not putting off..." coursed through his daily chores, high school classes and clubs, and athletic endeavors—he ran on the track and field high school team. He would eventually manifest this diligence in his college application to Morehouse College, where he was accepted and from where he eventually graduated. Even with numerous major setbacks and hurdles occurring, my brother went on to earn his master's degree from Xavier and his PhD in counseling and psychology. He now teaches in Washington, D.C., and I am continually impressed by his persistence and determination. The numerous accolades he has accumulated throughout his life are a reflection of the ways in which he has "not put off until tomorrow what he could do today." While all of my siblings heard this message over and over in our childhood, it resonated differently for my brother. The ways in which message repetition reinforces cultural values like work ethic can mean different things and have different impacts depending on factors like gender, sibling birth order, or even situations surrounding the message reception.

Messages like "don't put off until tomorrow," generally first attributed to Benjamin Franklin, recur throughout our culture. Many of us have heard similar messages because they reinforce shared cultural values like work ethic. By contrast, family messages also sometimes intentionally contradict or challenge common cultural values.

Parents may intentionally try to raise children to go against the grain, reject rigid concepts related to gender or sexuality, or embrace ideas that larger cultural groups have yet to take up. However, even when intentionally crafting messages that break with culturally endorsed values, we're acknowledging those values exist. Counter-messages and disruptive messages still acknowledge a common message that *needs* to be countered. There would be no reason to tell someone to "love their body" if we were unaware that young people are surrounded by messages telling them to hate their bodies. There would be no need for messages that instruct self-care and attention to mental health if we were unaware of the prevalence of burnout, mental and emotional exhaustion, and messages that otherwise endorse prioritizing productivity over one's well-being. There would be no need for messages encouraging one to be themself if it were not for the abundance of messages supporting conformity.

While we come to the table with memorable messages unique to us that help form our identities, support or challenge our individual relationships, and shape who we are, separate from those around us, we also come with so many shared experiences, collective, repetitive narratives, and cultural values repeated over and over through our memorable messages. That is why so many of us can recall the same or similar memorable messages. People who grew up within the same generation or region likely recall the same messages that were reflective of the larger culture's values—both good and bad. Part of the power that culture has on the value systems we adopt occurs through message repetition—hearing and seeing the same idea over and over again, often from many sources.

While messages stemming from cultural values do reflect what is important to a particular culture, that doesn't imply those messages are good or bad. We will get into how and what to do about memorable messages that help and hurt us later, but for now it's worth noting that culture doesn't imply a moral value—it is not inherently good or bad, it just is. Culture exposes us to many memorable messages that help us, form identities we take pride in, and establish productive practices that serve us or our family systems well. But sexism is also a part of culture. Racism is a part of culture. We receive plenty of culturally informed messages that can and do hurt us and warrant critically reflecting on and often rejecting. We highlight this to emphasize that our use of the terms "culture" and "cultural" here are intended to be descriptive, not evaluative.

In sum, messages are memorable because they are repeated, and that repetition occurs at both the individual and cultural level. Fully understanding, learning from, and challenging the messages that stay with us means examining how often we heard them, and how we feel about where we heard them from.

Before proceeding to the next chapter, we encourage taking another moment to reflect on some of those culturally repeated messages:

- What messages shaped important parts of who you are?
- What messages did you take from the media when you were younger? How about now?
- Did your family system support or reject the common messages you heard from the world around you?

In the next chapter, we'll explore another reason we find some messages memorable: because we use them. The messages we endorse and ultimately use become more memorable.

3

Utility

Do we find the messages we receive useful?

A considerable reason that messages remain memorable for us over time lies in their utility. We recall these messages because when we encounter situations in our life, we draw upon them for guidance or comfort. Utility is the first step in a message ultimately impacting anything, and the vehicle through which memorable messages affect our relationships, identity, and behavior. Not all messages that guide us throughout our life do so in a way that actually helps, strengthens, or improves our life. Recall, for instance, all the bad advice you might have received and, at some point, believed. Instead, utility refers only to whether or not we ultimately *use* a message, not *how* we use it. In this chapter, we'll explore how memorable messages, as a unit of communication, work as a tool in our lives. Like most tools, they can be used in ways that help or harm us. To illustrate the myriad ways that we use memorable messages, we each share three examples of messages that we found useful in our own lives. The first three stories come from Val, and the second three from Angela.

"Plan for the worst, and when it gets here, it won't be that bad."

Not all messages that are useful to us need to be delivered interpersonally. Sometime in my early school years, I read that line in a book assigned to me for class: "Plan for the worst, and when it gets here, it won't be that bad." I don't remember the story that landed that lesson, but I do remember the words well. Sometimes we hear something and immediately buy into it. That's what happened to me here. I think if I asked almost anyone who knows me to describe me, "planner" would probably make their list of adjectives. This phrase is one I invoke when life-planning for storms, or moves, or illness, or anything else. It's certainly a pessimistic saying, one that assumes something bad will ultimately happen. But life does happen—good and bad—and for me, preparation, to the degree one is able, has always helped it feel much easier when life indeed happens.

Advice like this that sticks with us over time does so because we buy it. When we endorse messages, recall them, and incorporate them into our identity and behavior, we actively use them. In that utility, they remain memorable.

"A stitch in time saves nine."

My very brief Google search suggests the phrase originated sometime in the 18th century, and may be falling out of fashion. The homily, a favorite of my mother's growing up, encourages the listener to take time to do something correctly or address a problem in order to save time down the line. This particular message, as one that stood the test of time, passed down through my family. I grew up hearing it from both my mother and my grandmother, and presumably, my grandmother heard it from someone before her.

My family certainly shared many other messages in my adolescence and young adulthood, but most of the words of wisdom my parents and grandparents attempted to bestow upon me never committed meaningfully to memory. While this message was also memorable because of repetition, both my mom and my Gram said it pretty frequently, I also recall it because it was ultimately useful to me.

Let me offer two extremely small-scale examples to demonstrate this idea of utility. Just yesterday, while cleaning my house, I noticed some dust accumulating on our kitchen fan. My first instinct, like probably a lot of us: let it go for now. But I encountered the memorable message passed down through the generations of my family: A stitch in time saves nine. Clean it now, or it'll be worse when you get around to it. Similarly, I call upon this idea every Sunday when I'm meal-prepping for the week. When grumbling to myself, annoyed about spending an hour of one of my days off engaged in a chore, I remind myself that this activity saves me several hours throughout the week. A stitch in time saves nine. Compared to some of the more identity-forming examples—such as how Angela's brother internalized a similar message ("don't put off") which motivated significant work ethic—that little phrase and that little moment might seem insignificant. But our lives are full of little moments. Words that actually move us to do anything, to think differently, to feel differently, or to behave differently, in ways that are big or small, matter.

"You're exactly where you need to be right now."

At 24, as I wrapped up my master's degree, I considered what to do next with my life. At the encouragement of a professor, I applied to a PhD program. Ultimately, I ended up waiting a year before pursuing my PhD at a different university. My parents encouraged me to move home for a year and join the service corps or work a local job. After six years of relative independence, the idea of returning to live with my parents for any reason bummed me out.

People who know me now would probably feel surprised to learn that any iteration of me ever faced uncertainty in life decisions. Ever since hearing "plan for the worst, and when it gets here, it won't be that bad" as a kid, my inner planner took over. I typically plan the next five years of my life at a time. When I began my MA, I intended to work in public relations, but after taking a research methods course, I fell in love with research and changed my mind while I was there. The shift in plans threw my very Type-A self into a spiral. When we're stressed and uncertain, we often draw upon advice people gave us in the past, or encounter new advice. Most of the advice I received then, as is typical for advice-receipt in most circumstances, was not useful to me at that moment. People compare situations that aren't comparable or claim to know how we feel when they rarely do.

However, one of my best friends, texting me late one night while I debated the next step in my life, shared a memorable message of her own with me. To this day, it remains one of the most useful messages I have in my self-care repertoire. At the time, my friend Meg went to yoga four or five times a week. She recounted that her yoga instructor always shared the message: "You are exactly where you need to be right now," and that she repeated it to herself sometimes when she experienced stress, and found it comforting. I also found it comforting.

To this day, I still repeat it to myself any time I feel overwhelmed or unsure. The reason this message has stuck with me for the last decade is because I have found it useful. In that moment of stress, the message grounded and calmed me, and in moments of stress since, I use that message to remind myself to be present and find meaning in the moment that I am in. For my very future-planning-oriented personality, a message that reminds me to find comfort in the present moment proves surprisingly useful.

"A closed hand cannot give anything away, nor can it receive anything, but much can flow in and out of an open hand."

Growing up, the basement of our tiny little home would often flood during the storm seasons. My stepdad took all sorts of precautions to ensure minimal damage, but the basement did not care. Each flooding would send the household—anyone at home—into a frenzy, running about with rags, a mop, and a bucket. On this particular day, the seemingly endless downpouring rain turned our neighborhood into a pond, spanning our full street and a grassy triangle-shaped field in the front of our home. Soon enough, water streamed from the basement windows.

While my siblings and I rushed to help my stepdad manage the basement, my mother, upstairs at the time, had opened the curtains of the large picture window in the front of our house to check on our neighbors. Amid our own chaos, a car and passenger stuck in the middle of the body of water drew her attention. She called my stepdad from his basement responsibilities and asked him to go out and get the person in the car, bring them into the house, and then call AAA to have their car towed out of its precarious spot. With much frustration, being distracted from his primary responsibilities—don't let the basement flood—my stepdad begrudgingly went outside to gather the stranger and bring them back into our home.

We all gathered at the window to watch. It turned out that the stranger, an elderly man, hadn't realized the waters were so deep and decided he could drive through them. Of course, he could not. When he got inside our home, my mother introduced herself, made us introduce ourselves, and shared our ages. I'm still not sure why that mattered. Then my mother, bold as ever, instructed my stepdad to get his robe and ask the elderly man if he would allow her to put his wet clothes into the dryer while we waited for AAA to come and tow his car. Oddly, the stranger agreed. After he changed into my stepdad's robe, she offered him a seat at our kitchen table, made him some tea, grabbed some of our store-bought cookies, and talked to him like he was a family member who had come for a long-awaited visit. I can still recall how puzzled I was that she'd done all this without one thought. She would later tell us that "closed hands cannot give anything away nor can they receive anything, but much can flow in and out of an open hand."

Making him feel welcomed and caring for his immediate needs only seemed what was expected. Understanding the give and take of caring for others informed my understanding of what being a part of a community means—making the message from my mother a useful one.

"Don't sweat the small stuff cause it's all small stuff—can't take it with you anyways."

I believe there was a reason my mother encouraged us to not get so wrapped up in our possessions or matters that she considered small or inconsequential. She often reminded us that "things" or "items" would come and go, but people were lasting. Fond of the popular saying "you can't take it with you," meaning that when we leave the earth one day, our possessions do not come with us. Instead, she encouraged prioritizing our relationships and connections.

Daily, she demonstrated this for my siblings and me by how she showed up for our community. She knew everyone on our street, even if just to have a short casual conversation with them. There was Mrs. Pitts, an elderly, widowed African American woman who lived next door. Two houses down lived the Gandys—an Indian couple who had a daughter who was my age—Robyn. Mr. Gandy was a doctor and he and his wife were always warm to my family. Then there were the Mitchells, a white couple with two sons close in age to me. I am sure if my mother were with me right now, she'd share how important it was that I got to grow up in a racially diverse neighborhood or how the members of the neighborhood held a variety of different occupations. But above their skin color, religion, or employment status, they were people and having relationships with them was what was most important in life.

Through this message, my mother emphasized that relationships were important and to be tended to with great care—certainly above things. So, in my childhood, when my neighborhood friends and I had a scuffle or got angry about someone breaking a toy or material items, as children often do, mom was quick to tell us, "Don't sweat it ... can't take it with you anyways." This seemed to calm us down and it always helped me move toward a solution. Sometimes, this led to pragmatic conversations about if a damaged object could reasonably be fixed. Some broken toys could be easily mended—you can put the chain back on a bicycle. Sometimes the items can't be fixed, but she would always resist the temptation to let the things, items, possessions of life overwhelm us. They were fleeting; relationships were not.

Similarly to the last message, I use this memorable message from my mother to remind myself to prioritize the relationships in my life. I use it to remind myself that the people in my life are far more important than material possessions.

"It doesn't matter what color the person is—they can be green or purple—what matters is that they love you; that you love each other."

As may be apparent, I understood multiculturalism, diversity, and inclusion before I knew what those words meant. It showed up in our home and community in so many interesting ways. My oldest sister, a true artist and creative sort of hippie, had dynamic dating relationships and eventually multiple marriage stories. She is 11 years my elder. Her story could be its own book, so for brevity here, I'll highlight that her choice of partners did not always please my mother. This memorable commentary, "It doesn't matter..." was likely part proverb and part warning to the younger of us. While my eldest sister didn't always have a well-rounded understanding of being loved, she did engage in a multitude of different relationships, maybe as a means to figure it all out. I believe my mother shared the above adage to let us know that love was most important, not the color of a person's skin or their size, shape or gender. My sister's first husband was white and my oldest nephew is biracial. Her next husband was from Africa. They didn't have children together. My sister's dating relationships were also varied, and I am sure I don't have any clue about the genders and sexuality of many of those relationships. But I remember that for me, my mother emphasized the importance of being loved, and being worthy of love as well as an extender of love when/if I got into a romantic, long-term relationship—something else my mother never pushed me into. It wasn't a problem to be single again. My mother emphasized that if I loved myself, loving others would not be hard.

I remember bringing my now husband home to meet my parents. Mostly, I remember they were shocked that he was Black (it wasn't yet the age of phone cameras, so their first meeting was also the first time they saw him). Because of my academic socialization from high school through to college, I'd been one of just a few Black people in most of my social spaces. Because my academic and professional social network had been mostly white people, my parents just assumed, without concern, that this would be who I'd gravitate toward—who I'd have a relationship with or marry. For my mother, it wasn't an issue or concern. Her only questions: did they love me; did I love myself? I found this message a useful reminder of what to value in relational partners.

Types of Utility

As our varied big and small moments of utility shared above demonstrate, we use memorable messages in myriad ways. The messages Val shared tended toward messages that were integrated into her personality, influenced her behavior, or brought her comfort and peace. These were useful to Val because they influenced specific decisions she made or helped her stay grounded and present. By contrast, Angela shared messages from her mother that she attributes to driving her core values of community, togetherness, and relationships. These messages were useful to Angela because they affect her relational choices in ways that she considers positive, and help her see herself in a loving light.

We can categorize utility by how it connects to all of the major outcomes of memorable messages: relationships, self-concept, and behavior. We find messages useful in ways that drive our behavior, help us assess that behavior, or affect how we see ourselves and others. Sometimes we use them simply by following the advice they contain (take time to do things right the first time; address problems as they occur, knowing it will save you time down the line; look someone in the eyes when speaking to them). Sometimes we use them by adopting the core belief into our personality or behavior (becoming a planner, embracing humility, valuing community). Sometimes we use them by finding comfort in them, realizing that they can calm us down or make us feel good (like reminding us that we are exactly where we need to be right now, or recalling the pride someone feels in us, or reminding us to love ourselves). We might find these messages memorable because they help us navigate a problem we face, promote healthy behaviors, or encourage us to keep going during hard times.

In fact, significant research has explored the relationship between memorable messages, resilience, and hope. Memorable messages, especially to the extent that the message is supported by other behaviors, can promote agency and direction toward resilience and hope that help us cope during tough times.[1] Most social scientists define resilience as the ability to bounce back from hard times and to use various resources (relying on people in our lives, navigating social programs, finding information) to sustain well-being.[2]

Memorable messages can help us develop those resiliencies. For example, an influential research study interviewed families who experienced financial difficulties during the economic recessions of the 1980s. In their study, they found that memorable messages about hard times help construct what the researchers called *short-term* and *long-term resiliencies*.[3] Messages like "tightening the belt" helped develop short-term resiliencies to make it through the initial financial crisis. Messages like "planning for the future" helped individuals and families develop longer-term resiliencies. That is, the kinds of family messages that stuck with people made them feel like they could make it through the crisis or helped them make decisions that got them through it. At the same time, families were sharing messages that they believed would help them prevent or cope with the next crisis.

Consider our own examples. Messages from Angela's mother

about the importance of community, valuing people over possessions, and embracing diversity can help inoculate an individual against more harmful experiences through the connections they have with others—their community. Or, by contrast, Val's message from her friend Meg—"You're exactly where you need to be right now." Messages like this may be useful because they provide comfort and help someone endure the present circumstances by finding meaning in their experience.

These messages operate to help us develop resiliencies in the present, but also to be able to anticipate the future. Memorable messages prepare us for challenges we may face down the line. The role of memorable messages in those anticipatory socialization experiences is to instruct us in what we should do or how we should feel about something that will occur in the future. For example, students may receive memorable messages for what to do when they struggle in a class before they have the experience of struggling in that class. Or people embarking on serious relationships might receive advice from people that tells them what to expect in a marriage and how to manage relationship or life challenges together. People receive messages that they feel will help them navigate sex, marriage, money problems, education, and many more life events. Research has looked at these kinds of messages in education, relationships, finances, and health, among other contexts.[4]

When fourth- or fifth-grade Val first read "plan for the worst," she did not bear the responsibility of engaging in any sort of actual planning. But that message instructed what she should do in the future when facing those decisions. Memorable messages can be useful by providing us with guidance on what to do when we are faced with decisions in the future. They can also be useful by helping us anticipate what sort of decisions we will face or what sort of experiences we will have.

For another example of how memorable messages are used to help us anticipate future circumstances, consider the messages you received when you were younger about romantic relationships. Maybe they occurred through observation—watching your parents, grandparents, siblings like Angela's reference to her older sister, or other adults in your life model their own relationships. Maybe they occurred through media—depictions of relationships on television or in movies, books, or social media. Maybe they occurred verbally—your mother telling you that "happy marriages take compromise," or that "relationships give life meaning." You likely received thousands of messages about relationships long before you ever even considered having one of your own.

Before you ever entered your first relationship, you carried memorable messages that told you what to expect, how to behave, what to tolerate, what to embrace, and what to reject. You had memorable messages that gave you a sense of where relationships fit into your life, the appropriate timeline for relationships to progress from casual to serious, the appropriate behaviors for a partner to engage in or display. You likely had what relationship scientists call implicit theories[5] about relationship success embedded in those memorable messages: "Relationships take work" or "If it's meant to be, it'll feel easy." Regardless of the content of those messages, you came to your first romance with ideas about it that were carried to you through those memorable messages. Whatever messages you invoked to form your expectations about dating, romance, or marriage were the ones that you ultimately used.

But we don't always use messages in ways that help us. Sometimes messages are used in ways that hurt us, or simply don't work in the situations we encounter in our lives. People also use messages that tell them they aren't good enough, or that they need to be perfect, or look or act in a way that doesn't work for them. Memorable messages can drive us to burn out, withdraw, or make harmful choices. For instance, some people come to dating with positive role models and messages about relationships that emphasize love and self-worth, but many people bring messages that discourage asserting their own needs, normalize degradation or violence, or instruct them to tie their value as a person to those relationships. Those messages hurt us, but we often use them anyway.

To be clear, message utility does not imply a moral value. We use messages in ways that don't ultimately serve us all the time, just as we use lots of things that don't ultimately serve us all the time.

We Use Messages We Endorse

The examples in this chapter demonstrate some of the ways we might use memorable messages, as well as an important condition of message utility: buy-in. In order for us to use a message, regardless of how we use it, at some point we have to endorse that message. We must buy in to some element of the message itself. The three messages each of us shared at the start of this chapter reflect just that. At least when we first heard those messages, we believed them. That might seem like an obvious statement, but unpacking the ways in which we buy into messages can help us disentangle those that no longer work for us, or that maybe need some updates.

When considering messages we have used, it's worth asking: did we use them in a way that actually helped us? Are we using them in ways that are actually *useful*? Perhaps a message helped us in the past, but doesn't work anymore. Or maybe one we used to think was helpful never actually helped us.

Take for instance someone navigating dating who has experienced some bad relationships in the past. To protect themselves, they might have heard messages regarding being careful about who they trust. Trusting people, after all, is how someone was able to hurt them in the first place. At one point, they might have used that message to protect themselves. But vulnerability is what grows relationships, and not trusting people also prevents closeness. They may realize that taking those risks is a part of life. Perhaps, when they first endorsed that message, that was what they needed to get through a tough experience and move forward. But as people grow and change and heal, that message eventually stops helping them and instead prevents new, meaningful connections with others.

We don't have to believe a message forever for it to be memorable; sometimes those messages change and adapt as we encounter life circumstances where the message no longer works for us. For instance, consider how one of Val's memorable messages changed:

Plan for What You Can

In 2021, we learned that my spouse, Sam, had an anaphylactic allergy in the way that many adults unfortunately learn it—their tongue suddenly and unexpectedly swelling, airways closing. I planned many things, and of course we had Benadryl in our house and my mom, a nurse, on speed dial, but that day still really sucked. I recall the trauma of watching a person I love more than anyone in the world nearly die, the pain on their face in the emergency room, and the chronic illness in the years since that massive inflammatory reaction was likely triggered. Planning for the worst might have helped, but it was still pretty bad.

This experience shifted a message for me in ways that the idealism and privilege of my youth had shielded me from: You can't plan for everything. Of course, not everyone has the ability to plan for every circumstance in the first place, and there are circumstances for which no amount of planning will prepare us. So, even though I felt my initial memorable message no longer worked for this perspective in my life, I still valued planning. Instead of rejecting the message, I adapted it: Plan for what you can.

Message Disruption and Adaptation

Val's story offers one example of what we call *message disruption*. This occurs when we encounter a life experience, a counter-message, or some circumstance that challenges or disrupts a memorable message we previously endorsed. Consider the earlier story Angela shared about her student's understanding of tampons. Her student grew up hearing that tampons would make her less "pure." Eventually, this student came to understand that was not true. While she did not share with Angela in that moment what ultimately shifted her perspective, we don't change our minds about deeply held beliefs for no reason. Something or someone shifts that perspective. That change agent is a form of message disruption. We might change our perspective because of an experience, as Val did in the story she just shared. Or we might change our understanding of a prior memorable message because of a new one. Perhaps Angela's student heard different messages from her friends once she went away to college and met new people. Maybe she learned information in a health class or read something online. Whatever form that message took, it became an act of disruption that undermined a previously held belief embedded in an earlier memorable message.

Messages are memorable because they are useful, but we don't have to passively accept how we use them. Throughout this book, we will make the argument that communication doesn't have to be something that just happens to us. We can be active participants in the process and take ownership of the messages from which we draw meaning, guidance, and comfort. They are a part of how we story our own experience, but it's important to remember to be our own storyteller.

Later in this book, we'll get into more detail and guide you through challenging your own messages that may benefit from some disruption. For now, let's think about some of your memorable messages and how they are useful to you. Try to list two or three of those messages.

Then, reflect on the following about those messages:

- How have you used them in the past, and how do you use them currently?
- Do they affect how you see yourself?
- Have they guided decisions you have made?
- If so, did they guide those decisions in ways that you found productive and helpful, or in ways you would do differently now?
- If you were delivering that message to yourself today, would you keep it as you first received it, or would you revise or adapt that message?

Next, we'll explore both an element of memorability and an outcome of memorable messages: relationships. We remember memorable messages because of who we hear them from, but they also impact our personal and professional relationships in many ways. First, we'll talk about how relationships affect a message's memorability.

4

Relationships

A common story we hear when collecting memorable message data or talking to folks about their own messages concerns our relationships with the people who sent them to us. Take for instance a common narrative in our research: A college student, when asked what memorable messages they recall about sex or sexuality, responds with something along the lines of "sex is bad," "don't get pregnant," or "only men enjoy sex." Then, the student quickly clarifies: "I don't actually believe that anymore, but I heard it growing up." If pressed why they still remember it, why it still sticks with them on the subject, a common answer is "Because that's what my mom told me."

Sometimes we remember messages because someone important to us delivered the message. Relationships, our connections with the people around us, interconnect with memorable messages, affecting the initial memorability of the message, and are affected by the messages.

People often tell us that they know one of their memorable messages, or many of them, contain ideas that might not be the most accurate or, in some cases, might actively harm them. So why do messages that we ultimately reject as invalid still matter so much to us? Why did we ever give them so much weight? While utility and repetition are a part of what make messages memorable, memory also stems from our relationship to the message source. Many of our childhood messages come from parents or other primary childhood caregivers; mentors such as teachers or religious or community leaders; older siblings; and grandparents. As we get older, memorable messages come from members of our important organizations and relationships such as the workplace, long-lasting friendships, and romantic partners.

Relationships are also an outcome of memorable messages—one of the reasons they matter and affect us. Our most memorable messages from a particular person can reflect the overall communication quality of that relationship. In Chapter 5, we'll explore how memorable messages affect relationship quality as an outcome of the messages. But in this chapter, we will discuss two other elements of messages and relationships. First, we'll talk about how relationships make certain messages memorable in the first place, wrapping up our discussion of how communication becomes memorable to us. Then, we'll talk about relationships as the *content* of memorable messages. Importantly, the discussions in this chapter and the next are separated for readability, but they ultimately inform each other and blend into one another.

We recall certain messages because the person who sent them to us mattered, but those same messages affect our relationship with that person. The connection between memorable messages and relationships can be thought of as bidirectional, with each end affecting and informing the other.

Relationships on Memorability and Behavior

Before we move into thinking about the many ways memorable messages and relationships connect, let's talk a little about how our relationship *to* a message source impacts whether or not we remember that message in the first place. That is, how does who a message comes from impact its memorability? A person's relationship with a message source affects message reception, or how we understand, interpret, and apply the message, in a few specific ways.

First, our relationships impact how we interpret a message. Thinking again about meaning as the core of what makes a message a message, what someone's words or actions ultimately mean to us is highly impacted by the relationship with the person who sent that message. An axiom among communication scientists is that communication has both content and relationship meanings.[1] That's an academic way of saying that in addition to the literal substance of a message, our relationship with the sender of the message affects how we ultimately interpret it—what meaning do we take from it?

For example, a memorable message someone might recall hearing from a parent is "It's okay to ask for help." The content dimension of this message, the substance, is that it is okay to ask for help. Literally, it refers to the message content. For verbal messages, that is pretty straightforward, but when we start looking at nonverbal messages, that content dimension can get messier. But that same message also has a relationship dimension. What's going on between the person who received this message and the parent who sent it? What's their relationship like? Those kinds of details help us understand if the message is one of support or of dismissal, one of affection or of hostility. If you have a good relationship with your mom, and you're struggling with something, you might interpret that message as a supportive one—a reminder that you're not in it alone. But if your relationship with your mom isn't so great, the message might sound dismissive, an assumption that you can't do something, or even come off as aggressive. How we ultimately make sense of the messages we receive is closely connected to how we feel about the person who sent them to us, and how we feel that message reflects the nature of that relationship.

Consider another example. Someone gets a new job that they're really excited about. They share the news with their friend in a text message. The friend responds "Congrats" without any punctuation or emojis. In the mediated world, punctuation or emojis can help fill in the reduction of other nonverbal cues, offering loads of ambiguity to how someone might ultimately decode even a simple message. Part of how the person who received that message will ultimately make sense of it has to do with their relationship with the other party. If this is a friend who they typically find is kind and supportive, who has a relationship history that leaves them with many memories of feeling welcomed and encouraged, then it is more likely they will understand that message means "Congrats" with an enthusiasm that simply can't be communicated as well via text message. Or perhaps they know from how this friend typically texts that they simply do not usually use a lot of punctuation to emphasize their points. Alternatively, if this friend has a more strained relationship with them, they recently had a fight, or they feel generally unsupported by them, they may read the word "Congrats" quite differently than its literal substantive meaning. Perhaps they feel the friend intends it sarcastically, dismissively, or is simply expressing congratulations for the purpose of social convention and not as a reflection of sincere enthusiasm for a friend's success. The many different ways we can interpret even a singular word is heavily swayed by relationship and context.

The relationship then impacts how we assign *intention* to messages. You can look at perceived intention as "what did they really *mean* when they said that or when they did that?" In reality, we usually don't know the answer to that question because we're not mind readers. But how we interpret that intention launches a ripple effect in our brains that concludes in how the message ultimately impacts us. To illustrate, Val recalls a memorable message from her college graduation:

Of the four graduations (and three ceremonies, I skipped my PhD hooding, don't tell) I experienced during my too many years of education, my undergraduate one is the most memorable. Twenty-two years old and packed into the Liacouras Center in Philadelphia along with hundreds of other graduates from the various degrees housed in my college, excitedly taking selfies with my best friend and waving at classmates and friends I spotted among the crowd, I half-listened to the commencement speaker offering us advice as we embarked on the next stage in our life journeys. Impossible to spot between the large crowd and my own vantage point, somewhere in the stands sat my parents, uncle, and his partner, eager to hear my name called. During the commencement speech, my dad texted me, "Your mom is crying."

My mom's a crier, so crying at big events is pretty typical of her behavior. Lovingly, my dad's text meant to tease my mom, but also to share the message my mom's tears embodied: "We're proud of you." I interpreted that message the same exact way two years later at my master's graduation, and two years after that when I published my first journal article, and again when I completed my dissertation and got married and saw her cry again, tears of pride and love at my brother's wedding just last year.

Tears can mean a lot of things. But I knew my mom's tears meant that she was proud of me. Tears, like many ambiguous nonverbal messages, could have meant that she was sad I was moving to Boston next instead of back home, or that she was wildly bored by the commencement speaker, or upset about something unrelated. I also could have perceived that the tears represented an exaggeration, something inauthentic that my mom performed for other people around us. But I didn't. I interpreted those tears to mean pride in her daughter, and believed they represented an authentic display of my mom's feelings. I felt this way because messages don't exist in isolation. The entirety of a relationship we have with someone leads us to interpret their messages the way we ultimately interpret them.

I interpreted another message here too, from my dad. Unlike my mom, who wears her heart on her sleeve, my dad is a little closer to the vest. He's more comfortable making dad jokes than expressing emotions directly. Although I don't remember the details, I'm sure he hugged me after the ceremony and told me he was proud of me, but I felt that the moment he shared my mom's tears expressed pride from him too. I assigned two meanings to my dad's text: He was teasing my mom, and he was proud of me too and wanted to share that pride with me in the moment (knowing that I was 22 at the time and most definitely glued to my phone throughout most of my graduation ceremony). I could have just assumed he was lovingly poking fun at my mom (and he most certainly was), or that he just wanted me to know my mom was proud. But I also interpreted my dad's message as his pride as well.

There are many ways that people say they love us, or they're proud of us, or they're here for us. But whether or not that's the message we ultimately interpret from a long, comforting hug, or "did you get home safe," or our mothers tearing up at important events has less to do with the message itself and much more to do with the relational history between the two people involved. Our relationship quality, the history of our relationships and their ups and downs, affects how we make sense of the messages we receive on every level. In this example, because Val had a loving and supportive relationship with her parents, she interpreted that message as reflecting their pride in her accomplishments. If someone had a more tense or difficult relationship with their parents, they might have interpreted the exact same words as a complaint, as performative or even irritating. That is because meaning lives in people, not in the words or behaviors alone, and people are relational.

Second, our relationships explain why we remember certain messages in the first place. We sometimes commit messages to memory *because* we value the relationship with the person who said it. We remember what our parents said about important features of life or pivotal life moments in part because they're our parents and what they said matters to us. It's also why we remember when someone important to us *didn't* say something we needed to hear. Consider an example from Angela about how her relationship with her mother led to remembering:

My mother taught me how to sew at a young age. Sewing would serve as a beautiful connection for us over the course of her lifetime. While working on sewing projects together, we had many meaningful conversations. I remember that she instilled in me how important it was to sew with attentiveness to whatever it was I set out to create. This included everything from picking out a pattern to the threads and the fabrics. She was insistent that I put care and thoughtfulness into the whole process because it would be something of value—made by my hands.

I recall a specific Christmas photograph; I believe I was six years old. While the tree that year was full of toys, clothes, and an Easy-Bake Oven, the gift I most cherished, which still remains on my top 10 gifts list, is the miniature electric sewing machine that my mother had to hunch over. In a photograph I still cherish to this day, she is showing me how to thread the needle on the machine and then sew on small pieces of fabric. As I look on attentively, I am told that this tiny machine was not equipped to handle large sewing projects, it needed to be treated delicately, and it was to teach me how to work on small items. I loved this tiny army-green sewing machine! It had just enough bells and whistles for my mother to teach me the primary steps like threading the machine, pressing on the foot pedal, and lining up a piece of fabric to sew. The memorability of this time for my first entry into learning to sew as well as the many sewing lessons I'd receive afterward bring such fond and enduring memories of learning to be confident in a skill from start to finish. I recall this gift, and this moment, because it was a meaningful exchange in the context of a close relationship with someone I cherished.

The people who matter the most to us are the same people we expect to fill our lives with important words of wisdom, comfort, or reassurance. For Angela, this was her mother. Her example of her mother teaching her to sew at a young age and then returning to that practice over the course of her life offers an illustration not only of instilling a skill set but of centering a mother-daughter relationship. The closeness of that relationship led to Angela continuing, to this day, to recall details of her mother teaching her. Her mother encouraged a work ethic, a care for the craft of sewing, an understanding that good work takes time, and a realization that everyone might not like the product, but if made by her hands, it still matters. Angela learned that what she created with her hands was to be valued and cherished—the innate value of our creations. These messages remain memorable to Angela in large part because her mother delivered them. Through her close relationship with her mother, she internalized those values and they became a part of how she sees herself and her relationship to things she makes.

Remembering a message because it came from someone with whom we had or have an important relationship is one element of the context that surrounds message enactment and reception.[2] That is an academic way of saying that the circumstances in which a message occurs—what's happening when someone says or does something, who they are and what their relationship is to you, why are you together in that moment in the first place—all of those details affect how we ultimately understand and interpret the message.

Relationships do not solely make up the context that affects message interpretation and memorability. A pretty large range of both internal and external factors also contextualize messages for us. We are more likely to recall memorable messages from transitional moments in life—when we're going through something, moving from one stage to another, starting or ending a relationship, or a job, or an educational endeavor—than from the important but sometimes less memorable day-to-day communication we have with people. While the situational context certainly also affects memorability, the person from whom we receive the message remains important. We expect the people we care the most about, with whom we hold the most enduring relationships, like family, close friends, or romantic partners, to show up and offer a sense of stability when the ground shifts beneath our feet. When those relational partners send the message we need, we tend to remember it. When they don't, we tend to remember that too.

Memorable Messages about Relationships

In addition to the many ways our relationships impact how we receive, interpret, and ultimately remember a message, the content dimension—what a message literally says—also often reflects relationships. To demonstrate, we'll each share some examples of memorable messages we received about relationships themselves. First, Val will share messages she received from her parents. Then, Angela will share messages she received from her mother.

"Relationships can be harmful."

Growing up, I recall my parents spending most Friday nights together. Even when they were busy, even when we were little and it meant paying the teenager who lived across the street to hang out with us for a few hours or persuading my grandparents to let us watch cartoons with them. Many times, my mom explained that they had their weekly date night, and she often shared advice along the lines of "It's important to make time for each other in a relationship." My parents shared many messages about what a loving relationship looked like and how they ought to be maintained by virtue of example.

I also remember another memorable message from my mother: Relationships can be harmful. My parents are still happily married, but they each came to their relationship in their mid–30s with a prior marriage behind them. I recall my mom sharing largely positive messages about her relationship with my father, and receiving countless socializing messages about what love and relationships could look like from their interactions with each other. But my mom's prior marriage before she met my dad was a different story altogether.

I am not sure how old I was the first time my mom recounted cowering in a bathroom while her ex-husband punched a hole in the door, triggering an immediate acknowledgment that she needed to leave that relationship, but I don't really remember ever not knowing that story. Speaking openly about relationship violence can feel taboo—like something you shouldn't tell your children. But I've always been grateful my mom spoke so openly about it. Although there's no specific phrase or saying that I remember, I remember the message—the meaning—that relationships that hurt us are not ones in which we should remain. I kept that message with me when I went through high school and watched friends struggle with abusive partners. I knew well, even as a teenager, that abusive relationships existed, and that we will never find a happy ending in them.

Another message accompanied words of warning about the possibilities of relational violence in my mom's memorable narrative: It's okay to talk about bad relationship experiences. Growing up, I thought my parents had an idyllic relationship. I can count on one hand the number of times I recall them fighting (which usually ended in laughter by the time it was done—over something silly like my mom putting too much butter on my dad's muffin). They openly expressed affection, spoke about each other in positive terms, and, as I noted, prioritized their weekly date nights. But they were not the only relationship I observed in my youth or early adulthood. Unfortunately, but not surprisingly given the prevalence of relationship violence, I saw plenty of relationships among friends and family that caused pain and harm to people I loved. I actually went on to conduct some research studies on the subject of how to talk about and disclose relationship violence to others because I so strongly believe it's a subject we need to talk more about to the people who matter to us.

I'm a relationship scientist, and I love "love" and relationships, and I know that healthy meaningful connection to others is what gives life meaning. But I also know how much harm relationships can and do cause many people. My connection to the concept of relationships and my engagement with many relationships in my own life started with two sets of messages I received from my mother about what relationships can look like when they bring us safety, warmth, and love, and what they look like when they bring us danger, harm, and hurt.

For those who know my mom, someone who walks right up to white supremacists to explain why they're wrong and stops to lecture anyone she hears making an offensive comment, the idea of her as a victim of anything would seem shocking. She's a tough person. It was hard for me to imagine any version of her that would ever be in that kind of relationship for even a minute. But precisely because my mom's a tough cookie, I took another message from her story: Relationship violence can happen to anyone; it's not a reflection of who you are.

To end this story on a perhaps humorous note, when I asked my mom's permission to share this experience here, she responded, "I've never been in an abusive relationship, what are you talking about?"

To which I quickly said, "You've told me a thousand times about your ex-husband punching a hole through the wall in your bathroom."

She said, and I quote: "Oh yeah, that guy."

My mom elaborated on this message I've held with me for a long time, sharing that this one incident had prompted her to leave. Knowing what abusive relationships looked like from other people in her life, she had no intention of remaining in one. My mom made sure to tell me that story when I was young so I would know what abuse looked like, and know not to tolerate it even just once.

"If a man puts his hands on you don't believe he won't do it again"

Like Val's mother, my mom's first marriage was embedded in domestic abuse. However, unlike Val's mother, my own mother's story, both simple and complicated, accompanied many nuances which I won't disclose here, all grounded in the era of "don't talk about it." During my own childhood and within that culture, abuse was something you didn't speak about. Out of necessity—financial support and housing—women typically stayed with their abuser. Some felt there were others who had it worse than them and on most days their partner was pretty good to them and their children. But my mom did leave the relationship and she did talk about it with me and my siblings. I've wondered often if, after divorcing this man, the time apart became the break that my mother needed to realize that no person, no man should put his hand on his partner.

I was not yet born, yet my older siblings still remember the fear of growing up with an abusive father. I know for a fact that because my mother knew well the experience of being hit by her first husband, she never wanted her children to go through similar experiences or be in such relationships. To that end, when we had conversations about relationships with our mother, while she spoke of the importance of mutual respect and love, she also warned us about signs of abuse. She warned us that if it happened just once, it would happen again.

The simple message carried in it a deep sorrow. She wished that her children would never have to experience the kind of pain that comes with abuse. It is easy to question why a person would let themself remain in an abusive relationship. What sort of messages, verbal or nonverbal, had they received? I never had an opportunity to ask my mother why she stayed as long as she did. I know that her father, who was a gentle, loving person from her description of him, died when she was a teenager and she was raised by her older sisters and brothers. I also know that my mother was in love with this very talented musician who was described as a sort of "bad boy." I also know he was prone to outbursts of anger and that he had a temper. Lastly, I know he, like many other Black males living through the 1930s–1950s, survived in a period of time known as Jim Crow where overt racism, violence, restrictions to education, and an array of other limitations formed the norm of the culture and climate. For instance, we now know that this period in our history had a profound effect on the mental and emotional well-being of Black men. There are so many "what ifs" or speculations to the story of his abuse toward his wife—my mom—but he did hurt her. The reality is that this dark time in my mother's life meant she was vigilantly perceptive about who her children had relationships with, especially intimate ones. Candid about the fact that there was no room for mental or physical hostilities (verbal or nonverbal) or abuse in those relationships, my mother emphasized that physical violence, if tolerated, would result in a cycle.

The reality of walking through life as women means that our mothers were far from the only people we knew or know who experienced abusive relationships. Relationship violence and emotional abuse remain horrifically common for people of all genders.[3] However, because these messages came from our mothers, they became memorable and influenced us in ways that many of those other messages did not.

Beyond memorability, our stories here highlight another important feature about these messages and relationships: message content. A lot of the messages we remember happen to be about relationships. If we think about it, that's not that surprising. Relationships make life meaningful, impact our mood in big and small ways, and revolve around many major life decisions and moments. Also, they're fun to talk about. We all have advice and experiences (good and bad) about relationships that we're eager to share with whoever wants to listen.

As relationships play such a central role in our emotional lives, we constantly search for ways to make sense of our own relational experiences. Most of us want words of wisdom that will explain a bad decision or mend a broken heart. A lesson we both took away from our mothers' first marriages was that sometimes relationships hurt people, but we also took away a diverse and varied profile of those who might experience relationship violence. These messages helped shape our intuitive feelings about what relationships can and should look like (and, importantly in the context of abuse, what they shouldn't look like).

Memorable messages about relationships, in part, inform the implicit theories we talked about in the last chapter. These theories describe a set of assumptions that we have about the way people operate,[4] including how people act and what relationships are like. For example, we might have an implicit theory that people are basically good, that personality is stable, or that relationships that are "meant to be" won't feel like work. These theories may or may not be accurate, but they are reflective of how we tend to feel about relationships and other people. These kinds of assumptions build a framework in our head for how we ultimately understand and evaluate others, including relationships. Memorable messages are a part of what builds that framework. When we internalize the messages we receive about relationships, they help form the key assumptions we hold about what relationships should look like.

Implicit theories are those held by everyday people, not theories in the way that scientists develop and test them. This means that our implicit theories are based on meaningful social experiences we've had, not necessarily drawn from research or science. But just because they may not be true in a scientific sense doesn't mean they aren't meaningful. Most of our belief systems do not stem from psychology textbooks; they come from the experiences we have interacting with the world around us and the messages we find memorable among those experiences.

"Relationships are about compromise."
"Dating around is normal."
"It's okay to rely on your partner, but don't be dependent on them."
"If it's meant to be, be patient."
"Good communication makes for good intimacy."
"Relationships should make you feel good about yourself."
"Respect one another."
"You should never feel trapped."
"If someone makes you feel pressured to do something you don't want to do, then they don't love you."
"Don't have sex before marriage."
"It's okay to have sex before marriage."
"Make sure they love you more than you love them."
"Relationships don't have to be sexual to be valid."
"Make sure it's not someone who hits or belittles you."
"Put your needs first."
"Put their needs first."
"Stay true to yourself. Don't ditch everyone else to date someone."
"Don't let anyone change you."
"Act dumber than you are; future partners may be intimidated by your intelligence."
"A good partner will wait for you to have sex."
"You should have enthusiastic consent."
"Relationships mean being at ease around one another."
"Open your ears first and your mouth second."
"Abstinence until marriage."
"Be cautious and don't trust men."
"Make sure to be attractive and pleasant."
"Always be honest."
"Your partner should consider your needs."

Like these examples and our mothers' warning stories, a lot of memorable messages are just *about* relationships. The messages above reflect some of the thousands shared with us through our research and presentations, real words that people report as their own memorable message about relationships. These positive, negative, and neutral relationally focused messages help us form implicit theories about what relationships are supposed to be like. They tell us what to expect or anticipate in the future, what to do within relationships, and how to make sense of good or bad relationship experiences.

Perhaps most importantly, they provide a comparison point that we judge our relationship experiences against. For instance, if Val's only memorable messages about relationships came from her parents' happy marriage, she might have formed an idealistic set of assumptions, leading to disappointment anytime she encountered relationship experiences that did not compare to that standard. But Val's parents' relationship was only one of a variety of memorable messages she received—demonstrating a diversity of relationship experiences that created a broader framework, including one that allowed for the possibility that she might meet or connect with people who would ultimately not be good for her.

Many common memorable messages about dating and relationships reflect traditional beliefs and assumptions about gender and sexuality, such as several of those above. As you may recall from previous chapters, a lot of these messages repeat through a variety of sources—TV shows, books, movies, celebrity culture, social media—but parents, grandparents, older siblings, and religious or community leaders also share messages about relationships with us. Sometimes we take these messages from observations or experiences—seeing what their relationships look like or hearing them comment on other people's relationships. Sometimes we get them because these people in our lives verbally share them with us. For instance, Val's example from Chapter 2 focuses on sexual orientation messages, but orientation is only one element of our sexuality. We also often receive messages about sexuality that encourage women to make their needs and desires smaller. Messages like "sex is for men" or "women don't enjoy sex" are also innately about relationships and how we experience relational intimacy in our lives.

A lot of our own research explores these kinds of messages that instruct women to understand relationships and express sexuality in narrow ways tied to strict gender roles. Research studies both from more than a decade ago[5] and from within the past year[6] report memorable messages that present a double standard, telling men to play the field or understand their role in relationships solely as a financial provider. Women report messages that direct them toward motherhood, encourage a pretty limited relationship with their sexuality, and instruct them to put other people's pleasure and experience before their own.[7]

Messages about gender and sexuality often reflect these really rigid binaries—ways of thinking that suggest options are black and white without considering the rainbow of colors or any shades of gray. A lot of these messages suggest the only options are man, woman, heterosexuality, and reproductive-oriented relations. While these obviously fail to account for many experiences that people actually have in the real world, they also provide a point in our brain for comparing the experiences we *do* have to these often unrealistic or limiting ideas about sexuality and relationships.

In later chapters, we'll elaborate on how memorable messages inform our behavior—how they influence us, or affect what we see as reasonable choices to make in our day-to-day and relational lives. Relationships are made up of choices we make as communicators. Memorable messages provide an important reference point for what choices we believe are actually available to us.

Having had some time in this chapter to think about the messages we receive about relationships, let's work through some of your own. First, take a step back and consider what assumptions you hold about relationships. What are your own implicit beliefs?

- What do you think the purpose of relationships is?
- What do you value in relationships?
- How should you be treated within a relationship and how should you treat others?

Take some time here to document your own relationship assumptions:

Now, consider what messages or memorable experiences helped form those assumptions. Basically, where do you think those ideas came from? The more detailed you can be, the more you'll get out of the exercise. Spend some time here really digging deep—why do you hold the assumptions you documented above? What experiences or messages led to them?

Briefly, do you believe those assumptions have been helpful or unhelpful to you as you navigate relationships in your own life?

So far, we have talked about how relationships with the message source impact a communication's memorability, and how many memorable messages are just about relationships. In the next chapter, we'll continue discussing relationships. We will focus on how memorable messages both affect and reflect the quality of our relationships.

5

Relationships as an Outcome

How Messages Affect and Reflect Who They Came From

Three factors primarily contribute to whether or not we ultimately recall a specific message over time: (1) how often the message is repeated either by the same source or through multiple sources; (2) how useful the message is to us either when we heard it or later on; and (3) our relationship with the person who sent us the message. These three elements elevate the many individual messages we receive throughout our life to "memorable" messages—the ones we actually remember and hold onto.

Now that we've spent some time establishing what memorable messages are and how they come to be memorable, we will be discussing what those messages do to us in more detail. Memorable messages matter because they affect us in a variety of meaningful ways. We categorize the outcomes of a memorable message, or what one does to us, along the dimensions of identity, behavior, and relationships. Memorable messages affect our sense of ourselves and the identity scripts and anchors we develop. They provide guides for assessing our behavior as well as directly influencing the behavioral choice we make. And they impact the quality of our relationships and the choices we make within those relationships. Since we are on the subject of relationships, we'll start there.

In this chapter, we'll continue our discussion about relationships and memorable messages by elaborating on how specific messages impact the overall quality of a relationship—how close we are with someone, how satisfied we feel with that relationship. We will

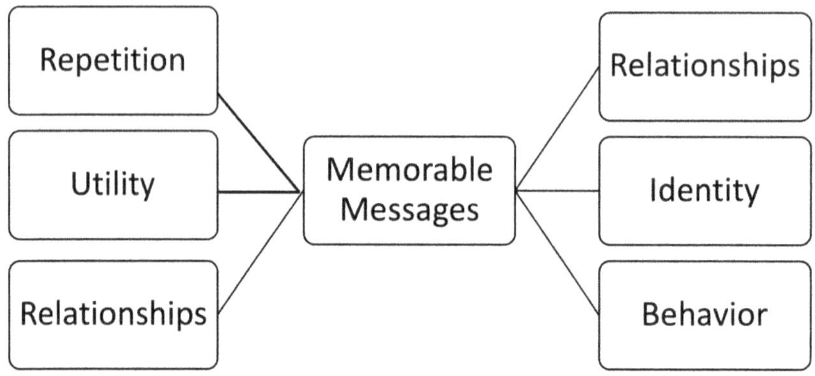

A model of memorable messages.

also talk about how the long-term transmission of memorable messages is affected by relationships, and how memorable messages move throughout generations of family.

Memorable Messages Impact Relationship Quality

Memorable messages, like all forms of communication, impact relationship quality. They can reflect and affect how we feel about a person. A popular Harvard University study[1] tracked what makes people happy over the last 80-plus years. Their findings overwhelmingly demonstrate that our relationships with the people close to us and our connection to our communities, more than money, genes, or anything else, are what makes us happy in life.

Relationships provide emotional and tangible support, meaning, comfort, and love. Relationships matter. But they can also seriously hurt us. Much of what makes relationships good or bad, satisfying or unsatisfying comes down to the quality of communication within those relationships.[2]

Unsurprisingly, then, as a particularly meaningful unit of communication, the memorable messages we receive from others can also affect our relationships with the person who sent them. Anecdotally, a lot of what we've shared in this book so far reflects that. You can see how our stories about lessons and messages we received from our mothers over time might make us feel more positively about our moms. But research also supports this.

For example, in a research study about the types of memorable conversations parents have with their adolescent children about sexual health, young people rated parents as being more effective communicators when they delivered more comprehensive messages—messages that covered more content and weren't overly simplistic.[3] Another study found that people who rate their memorable messages more positively are typically more satisfied and closer to the message source than those who think of their messages more negatively.[4] That means when we recall more positive, hopeful, and comforting memorable messages from someone, we feel closer to that person and better about the relationship overall. Different types or categories of memorable message affect how supportive we feel people are and our relationship satisfaction with those people.[5]

This should not come as a surprise, since how we communicate with others in general affects our relationships with them. Memorable messages form an important unit of communication, thereby holding a role as one of the factors in how that communication affects our relationships. Generally, research finds that messages that are more supportive, positive, and comprehensive lead to better evaluations of the person who sent the message. Memorable messages that are more dismissive, limiting or incomplete, or negative lead to more negative evaluations.

Features of supportive, positive, and comprehensive messages include affirming communication. Validating messages, like telling someone their feelings make sense, expressing positive feelings like declaring love, liking, or support generally result in more positive emotional responses toward the message sender. Messages that make us feel heard and understood include both verbal and nonverbal elements. These messages involve not only the words someone said, but whether or not they engaged in the nonverbal behaviors that made us feel valued and listened to: giving us their attention, perhaps putting a phone away or face down, nodding and looking at us while we speak. These seemingly small behaviors add up to send important messages that we remember over time, and help determine whether or not the same verbal message ("That sounds tough") might come off as dismissive and uninterested or validating and supportive.

By contrast, some people send messages that overtly hurt or invalidate the message receiver. When someone doesn't make time for us when we need it, that can also become memorable. Features of hurtful verbal communication tend to revolve around two forms of what researchers call *devaluation*, which means that the message makes us feel less valuable in some respect. Specifically, messages that devalue us as an individual or as a relational partner feel especially hurtful.[6] Individually devaluing messages include statements or perceptions that target personal characteristics—for instance, criticizing someone's personality or appearance. These messages feel hurtful because they communicate that the message sender does not value the recipient. Similarly, messages that devalue us as a relational partner—or that imply we are not as close or cared for as desired—also feel hurtful. For example, not being on the same page about relational commitments can elicit hurt feelings if one party wishes to date exclusively and the other party is not as serious. Or, for an established relationship, transgressions like infidelity that devalue the relationship can send strong and memorable hurtful messages. Even in family relationships, if a parent prioritizes other relationships or their work over time with their child, that may make the child feel devalued and hurt in that relationship.

But not all negative communication is overtly hurtful. We often encounter subtle messages that we could reasonably interpret in a number of ways. Nonverbal behavior (does someone appear to be invested and paying attention or do they seem distracted and disinterested), relational history (do we generally feel close and supported by this person), and communication context (what is going on in that moment and is it conducive to more intimate or more effective communication) all affect our ultimate interpretation and recollection. It's important to remember that how we make sense of those messages—the meaning we derive and remember—is always an interpretation. That interpretation and evaluation of a message as generally positive or generally negative impacts us and our relationships in real ways.

In the most basic way, that makes sense—when we receive

multifaceted, supportive, and uplifting messages we are more likely to feel positively about the person who sent them than we are if they sent messages that were dismissive or mean. However, that relationship isn't always linear or straightforward. In the case of our close relationships, we receive many messages from the same source. This might explain why sometimes relationships we still feel positively about can get away with delivering more negative messages. Or why we sometimes come to appreciate or understand a message that is less overtly positive at the time of delivery.

Close, ongoing relationships can handle the occasional message that isn't as positive or supportive—either because we needed some tough love in the moment or because our relational partner was having an off day. We draw from the compilation of all of those messages and moments when evaluating our close relationships. While memorable messages may hold special significance in our overall relational evaluation, a singular message, with only a few exceptions, rarely dictates the quality of a relationship alone. Memorable messages instead tend to reflect the general communication climate within a relationship. That is, when we think of the memorable messages we received from specific people in our life, they tend to be representative of the general quality of that relationship. If we recall messages that are loving and supportive, that is likely because we would typically evaluate that relationship as loving and supportive. If we recall messages that are mean and dismissive, that is because we are likely to evaluate that relationship as mean or dismissive.

Memorable messages impact the quality of those relationships. Communication is the medium through which relationships occur. When our communication is affirming, those relationships generally improve. But memorable messages also reflect the relationships—what we remember tends to represent the relationship overall. In that way, memorable messages both affect relationships—directly impacting the quality and closeness we feel to someone—and reflect them—providing representative moments for us to recall when we think about the people in our lives.

Relationships are also impacted by memorable messages over time. Many messages reflect family identities or may be transmitted across generations. Angela will share a story about the generational transmission of memorable messages within her own family.

Generational Memorable Message Transmission

In our household, family genealogy was an important point of pride. From it came stories shared by my uncles and aunts about those who'd paved the way for us to be where and who we were. One of those people was Thomas "Ty" Stokes—he was a famous Black cowboy and rodeo bull rider in the early 1900s. Before we had photos or Ancestry.com to validate this history, my mother kept a handwritten note that she'd pull out to show the grandkids to remind them that not only did we have an important family relative, but that he was a rodeo star. It is believed that he was my grandmother's brother. Ty was born in 1883 in Casey, Kentucky. It is documented that "though he died at the age of 46 following an operation, Ty lived a life full of adventure and daring in the early 1900s as a cowboy, bronco rider, trick rider and rodeo clown."[7] He was said to be "the best in the business of breaking wild horses and caring for race stock."

I always found it empowering to hear my mother share this story. It was typical for my mother to share stories about Ty when we talked about accomplishments or when she encouraged a "can do" attitude. Stories that passed through my family for more than a century underscored and contextualized memorable messages about what we were capable of. This generational transmission of messages meant that all family members needed to recognize that there were many known and unknown bridge-builders who had paved the way for us to have success and accomplishments. If our great-uncle could travel across the country on his horse, work in demanding conditions, deal with the discrimination afforded to a Black cowboy of the time, and then have the capacity to become a rodeo bronco rider and trick horse rider ... well, we had no right to complain or believe that we couldn't take on the smallest challenges in our lives.

As demonstrated by Angela's family tales of cowboy capability, another role relationships occupy involves what social scientists call the *generational transmission of memorable messages.*[8,9] Messages can last through the generations, shared by your parents with you, and your grandparents with them, your great-grandparents before them, and so on. Undoubtedly altered by the telephone game of time, given different weight, value, or meaning, we still repeat, remember, and feel affected by the messages that last throughout generations of family.

One of our own research studies,[10] led by a group of Latina women, looked at how memorable messages occurred across three generations of women in Latina and Hispanic families. For Latina women, health messages from family members often hold significant meaning, particularly those that transpire between grandmothers, mothers, and daughters. In these studies, our friend Ashley Aragón and her team examined the exchanges between tri- and multigenerational Latina women in the family system, focusing on reproductive and sexual health. Findings from the study emphasized the need to explore whether and how transparent, honest, and nonjudgmental conversations can foster a culture of mutual respect and openness among women in the Latine communities as they navigate their sexual behaviors.

Younger women valued the messages their mothers and grandmothers passed down to them, but often questioned the applicability to their current circumstances.[11] Even in instances where, as with the earlier story of Angela's student, the younger member rejected her mother or grandmother's memorable message, they still recall and are affected by it because they value their relationships with the message source.

While family relationships and repetition of these messages over time impact their memorability, even in cases where they may be less useful, these intergenerational memorable messages also impact our relationships and family identities. As Angela's story demonstrates, families may evoke these narratives over time to establish important values they hold—like drive and perseverance. They may also serve as lessons to socialize us into the world, inspire us toward resilience during hard times, or establish our value within the family[12]

For another example, in 2010, Dr. Jody Koenig Kellas, a communication and relationship scientist specializing in family storytelling, completed a research study on what she called the transmission of relational worldview through memorable messages.[13] Dr. Koenig Kellas looked at the relationship between mother-daughter memorable messages and adult daughters' romantic relational schemata, or relationship worldview, which is basically just the way we think about relationships—they're the structures in our mind for organizing, remembering, and interpreting messages related to relationships. The details you documented in the last chapter about your own relational assumptions during the last exercise form the basis for your own relational schemata. For example, some people might have assumptions that marriage means a couple shares everything, while other people might have assumptions that marital couples should still retain financial independence.

This researcher wanted to see if the memorable messages women recalled from their mothers about relationships affected their overall perception of relationships as adults—their relational worldview. Essentially, she wanted to know if memorable messages affect that overall view of a relationship. One of the ways meaning is transmitted from one generation to the next is through stories and messages, and Dr. Koenig Kellas's study sought to test the extent to which it was actually happening in the context of romantic relationships.

First, she found that memorable messages about relationships often reflected a few basic themes. One theme included messages that instruct the listener to value themselves or their independence, tell them not to settle, or encourage more progressive views related to sexuality, dating, and relationships.

Second, she identified messages focused on the characteristics of a good relationship. These described the qualities of a good partner (in this particular study, usually "a good man," but other research has elaborated on this in other directions), behavioral expectations for a relationship such as what to do if you're angry or hurt in a relationship, and the importance of finding someone similar to you.

The third type of message focused on warnings. In this study, these included general warnings (like "don't trust boys"), stories of the mother's personal regret, and judgments or expectations of women and girls. In other memorable message research, women receive stories of warning for a variety of reasons, including those that sort of normalize experiences like assault or violence.[14] Warning messages in general are common when passed between women of different age groups or statuses. The examples both of us shared of our mothers' experiences with domestic violence in the last chapter also serve as warning messages.

Lastly, messages contained the idea of valuing the sanctity of love. These were more traditional messages about waiting for marriage to have sex, believing in soul mates or "the one," and valuing marriage. A lot of the examples from our own research tend to reflect these more normative ideals.

Historically, three basic relationship schemata or worldviews exist: independents, traditionals, and separates. *Traditionals,* first defined by a scholar named Fitzpatrick,[15] describe a typical or conventional approach to marital relationships—viewing them as relationships that should be extremely intertwined with little individuality or independence. Relationship research describes that idea as highly interdependent—meaning their individual selves mutually rely and influence each other to a high degree. Historically, folks who endorse more traditional relational worldviews also follow traditional social conventions surrounding marital relationships, such as gender norms, who takes whose last name, marital timing, and how finances ought to be shared.[16]

Independents still believe in a high level of connectedness or interconnection with their marital partners, but may hold less conventional beliefs about what marriage is or what it should look like. Independents, as the name suggests, value more independence, "me time," and hobbies or interests outside of the relationship.[17] They may also be more open to relational roles that are less closely tied to gender norms. For instance, they may be more comfortable in a heterosexual relationship with the woman as the breadwinner, or same-sex couples may embody this schema. While independents value togetherness and couple time, they may also be more likely to each have their own hobbies, friends, and interests.

Lastly, *separates* hold what researchers describe as two opposing views on relationships—one that endorses traditional beliefs about marriage, and one that strongly values their own personal autonomy or independence.[18]

In Dr. Koenig Kellas's study, adult daughters who reported more memorable messages related to valuing themselves were 4.62 times more likely to have an independent relationship schema than a traditional one, and those with an independent schema in general reported more value self-messages than warning messages. Those with more traditional relationship worldviews reported more of a mix of messages, rather than value self-messages. This means that the types of messages we receive about relationships might influence our general view or orientation toward relationships, especially regarding how we think significant romantic relationships should basically function.

This study also looked at whether or not daughters thought they would pass those messages onto the next generation, continuing that generational transmission of messages about relational worldview. Dr. Koenig Kellas's study answered that question as: Maybe. For folks who received messages that were more positive about the characteristics of a good relationship, some were willing to pass them on. But those who received warnings or other more negative messages were less likely to report wanting to pass those messages on to their own children.

Let's consider a few takeaways from this and other memorable message research looking at how messages are passed down between generations:

1. First, the memorable messages shared with us about relationships reflect the value system of the person sending the message. That is, how people feel relationships should fit into their own life and the larger culture are embedded in even relatively simple messages about relationships. For someone who values independence or who had good or bad relational experiences that influence how they view relationships, those ideals and values become embedded into the messages they share with others.
2. Second, messages about relationships often turn into messages about families. This might occur because a message passed down through multiple generations of family—from great-grandparent to grandparent, grandparent to parent, parent to child—continues to feel relevant over time. It might occur because the message helps establish a family's culture or identity, or reinforces the role of romantic relationships within that family system.
3. Third, family and relationships and the messages we receive about them also reflect larger cultural messages. The messages we hear repeated in the media or read in books or see depicted in the relationships we witness out in the real world all influence how much weight we give to the messages we receive and those we choose to endorse or pass on. The messages individuals and families share also reflect larger cultural values. Consider our earlier chapter on

message repetition and how cultural values become transmitted through memorable messages when repeated through multiple sources. Many cultural values revolve around relationships, and the intergenerational transmission of memorable messages is a part of how those values persist over time.

Consider the messages that have circulated through your own family. Are there any messages you heard from a parent or caregiver that you believe they heard from their parent or caregiver?

Do those messages reflect your family identity? How do they make you feel about your family members and your relationship to them?

Would you pass on any of those messages yourself? Why or why not? In what ways would you change the messages if you were to deliver them to the next generation?

In the next chapter, we continue this discussion by exploring the impact of memorable messages on identity. We describe and share examples of how memorable messages shape who we are and how we see ourselves and invite you to consider how the messages you receive form and inform your own self-concept.

6

Identity

Over the past few months while writing this book, Val has compiled letters of support for her tenure case at her university. In a few of those letters, people she admires as professionals mentioned something along the lines of "she's a good writer." If you've made it this far in this book, we hope you agree. But the most recent professional endorsements follow a series of messages Val has received throughout her life, praising her way with words. The first memorable message about writing that Val still recalls came from her third-grade teacher, who told her on enough occasions that it sank in: "You're a really good writer." Within a year, Val dreamed of jobs in journalism or other professions that focused on writing, as many of us do, attaching to the endorsement of someone influential in her life.

As we've discussed, the message that formed a part of Val's self-concept in such a significant way was memorable and impactful not just because she heard it once from one important person, but because other people repeated the message to her over and over. In seventh grade, Val recalls her social studies teacher suggesting she enter a statewide essay contest. She won her first computer in that competition. In high school, her communication teacher asked her to help revive and edit the school newspaper. In her undergraduate program, she worked for the school paper and won awards for her writing. Now, writing is a part of her professional life and so embedded in her sense of self that she often notes that writing is how she thinks.

In graduate school, a professor told Val that he rarely understands how he feels about something until he's written it out. Adding to Val's existing compilation of memorable messages about writing, that message infiltrated her existing self-framework as a writer. The memorable message from an elementary school teacher encouraging a nine-year-old's interest shifted from "you're pretty good at this" to a lifelong approach to a craft. But if no one had ever shared those messages, Val might have felt less confident sharing her writing, which in turn would mean receiving less feedback and fewer messages that reinforced her relationship to it. Or, if the messages had been discouraging instead, if she came to associate a reception of her writing with negative feedback, she likely would not connect "writer" to her identity.

This experience demonstrates some of the ways that memorable messages influence our self-concept. Memorable messages shape, reflect, and reinforce our identity by offering templates or scripts for self-concept—the roles we play in our lives—and providing ideas about the self that anchor us or offer a sense of stability.

The childhood memory of "you're a good writer" came at a particularly meaningful moment for Val. The same year, one of her cousins, a college student at the time, ended up contributing to the release of a wrongly incarcerated person through her school's investigative journalism classes. Val vividly recalls her mom reading her the newspaper article sharing her cousin's accomplishment in helping to free an innocent person. Enchanted by the idea that writing could right wrongs in the world, coupled with recent praise from someone she admired that she too was a pretty good writer, little Val set out to write.

Researchers of memorable messages describe the backdrop within which we receive these messages as the *circumstances surrounding message enactment and reception.*[1] This is an idea we briefly introduced earlier in the book. It's a pretty academic way of saying that what was going on at the time we received a particular message might make it more or less impactful—basically, context matters for communication. Val's teacher probably praised the writing of several other students who did not ultimately incorporate that praise into their self-identity like Val did. So what happens that leads us to incorporate messages about how other people see us into how we see ourselves?

Memorable messages impact our self-concept in both positive and negative ways by enhancing our self-esteem or self-worth, making us feel like we can accomplish things, or encouraging and promoting resilience—or by discouraging us, putting us down, or making us feel like we can't do certain things. As we have discussed in previous chapters, these messages are more likely to be memorable and impactful when they are repeated, reinforced by social experience, and shared by someone whose opinion we care about. Under the right circumstances, memorable messages form the ideas about ourselves that anchor and stabilize us during times of stress or uncertainty. Memorable messages also reflect social or cultural identities and our connection to or distance from them. Let's start with some basic ideas about self-concept.

Self-Concept and Personal Identity

Because our memorable messages often come from the important people in our lives at important moments, we attach to them. These messages influence how we see ourselves, otherwise known as our self-concept. Before we dive into the important aspects of memorable messages and how they inform and impact our self-concept, we invite you to consider your own. What memorable messages have you received that reflect the ways you see yourself?

If you struggled to come up with messages that reflect how you see yourself, you can take a step back and just ask: How do I see myself? Who am I? Writing down notes, phrases, words, feelings, or moments that connect with your vision of yourself is a helpful starting point. From here, consider: Why do I see myself that way? What happened that led me to think this? This is where the memorable messages fit in—what did you experience that validated or undermined your ideas about yourself?

For instance, in Val's story that opened this chapter, messages that encouraged her as a writer offered positive feedback and validation from people whose opinion she valued (teachers and mentors). But "writer" isn't the entirety of Val's self-concept. She sees herself as calm, thoughtful, kind of nerdy, a person who wants to help other people, funny, and definitely a little neurotic.

Like all of our self-concepts, we see ourselves reflected back in other people through how they treat us, the messages they share both verbally and nonverbally, and the experiences we have that shape us. This concept is called the looking-glass self. A part of how we learn who we are is by seeing what others reflect back to us.[2] One of the reasons memorable messages are important is because they have the power to shape how we see ourselves and how we experience our sense of self. We encourage you to reflect on how those memorable messages contribute to your self-concept.

- Did your messages shape how you see yourself professionally, or your career trajectory?
- Did they shape how you see yourself in relation to others?
- Did they make you feel good about yourself, or maybe not so good?
- Did they make you feel like you're capable and competent, or like you're unable to do or accomplish something?

The word "identity" covers a lot of ground. To simplify it, we can think of identity in two major categories: personal and social. *Personal identity* is what we're talking about here—our sense of self, what sets us apart from other people. What are the features that make you a unique person distinct from those around you? We can contrast this with *social identity,* which refers to shared elements of identity associated with social and cultural groups like race, gender, religion, sexuality, region, or language culture, among others. This is how we identify with and through the groups and communities to which we belong.[3] We'll talk about how memorable messages relate to both personal and social identity in this chapter, but let's start off with the personal.

Personal identity involves how we see ourselves—or our self-concept. As humans, we have a basic need for self-esteem or a sense of self-worth.[4] But our sense of self, and related senses of self-worth and self-efficacy (which means feeling like we're capable of accomplishing things), don't appear out of nowhere. Starting in early childhood we receive messages about what we're capable of and why, what we're good at, what we're bad at, what's safe or unsafe to try, if we're smart, attractive, likable, and all the other ways that we are similar to or different from those around us. Who we see ourselves as, the good and the bad, is a compilation of messages and social experience received throughout our life, with a heavier weight given to messages received during early adolescence or during major life events and transitions.[5]

Many memorable message research studies have explored self-esteem as an outcome variable. This means that research has considered if and how the memorable messages we receive have an impact on our overall self-esteem.[6,7,8,9] Across several contexts, the types and valence (how positive or negative a message is) of memorable messages do appear to relate to an individual's self-esteem. It's important to note with these, and most memorable message studies, that the design of this research relies on an individual's recollection of their past experiences. This kind of data collection makes sense to understand the real-world implications of how we recall and use memorable messages. However, it has an important limitation that it is correlational, not causal, data. This means that we cannot definitely say that memorable messages were the cause of the change in self-esteem, just that there is a relationship between memorable messages and self-esteem.

Although self-esteem can change throughout our lifespan due to significant transitions or challenges we might face, or even especially meaningful communication with others, once we have developed our general sense of self-esteem in adolescence it tends to be relatively stable for most of us until later in life, barring significant life events. However, for some of us, even smaller-scale individual interactions can have a more meaningful impact on self-esteem.

Researchers call this idea *contingent self-esteem*, which describes self-esteem that relies on either self-imposed or other-imposed standards, which may be more likely to fluctuate within interactions.[10] For example, for most people, a coworker criticizing their work would not drastically affect their overall sense of self. It may put them in a bad mood, or leave them feeling upset with the coworker or interaction, it might even put a damper on the whole day, but it probably wouldn't seriously change how they see themselves. But people who have higher contingent self-esteem may have a less stable sense of self-worth,[11] which can be problematic, and leaves their self-concept more easily influenced through the communications they have with others. So, for such an individual, that interaction may leave them feeling particularly bad about themselves.

Self-esteem, like many of the more stable elements of our personality that can impact our self-concept, starts to develop when we're pretty young. The many factors that contribute to self-esteem fill entire academic journals, but memorable messages do make the list. Memorable messages as reflections of relational quality with our early caregivers can promote a sense of safety, security, and resilience that contribute to an individual developing a healthy sense of self-worth, or they can make us feel insecure, undermined, or incapable—depending on the messages.

It's important to remember that memorable messages can impact our self-esteem and our self-efficacy.[12] The first researchers to introduce the concept of memorable messages back in 1981 highlighted that they often provide positive, emotionally supportive, or reinforcing messages that help establish an individual's positive self-esteem.[13] When messages tell us "you're good at this" or "you can do it" or "you are very capable" in one way or another, they provide positive feedback that informs our self-concept. When we receive these messages from people who are important to us, or who were responsible for significantly socializing us like parents and teachers, they help inform our sense of self in ways that are positive and productive.

But we don't always hear positive messages. Plenty of our own research has explored the negative memorable messages people get about identity and relationships. But even at a more basic level, not everyone is told they're smart, capable, kind, or good at things. Some people receive messages that tell them they're "not smart enough for that," or instruct them to aim lower, to try something easier. Some messages prepare people to fail or anticipate pain and disappointment. These messages also affect our self-esteem and self-efficacy, just in a less positive direction. When negative messages are repeated, they can be internalized, meaning that the person believes them to a point where it affects how they ultimately see themselves. These negative self-related expectations can influence our future interactions and decisions.

Through personal feedback and experience throughout our lifetime, we develop a sense of who we are, separate from others. All of these elements compose our personal identities. But we also understand our identity in terms of our relationships to other people and the social and cultural groups to which we belong.

Relational, Social, and Cultural Identities

In addition to the messages that set us apart from other people—that reinforce or evaluate aspects of our personality (that we're funny, kind, or guarded) and individual capabilities (that we're smart or athletic)—we also receive messages that tell us where we fit in with other people. Messages about our various social identities, including cultural identities and relational identities, also shape how we see ourselves and fulfill our need for self-esteem.[14]

The first story Val shared in this book, "In this family, we help people," accomplished instructing Val to see herself as helpful as an individual, affecting her self-concept, but also explained a characteristic of Val's family identity. Messages about what it means to be a part of a family or to take up a specific role within one's family also inform our identity in a number of ways. If you consider the important roles you occupy in your life, familial and relational roles are likely pretty high on the list. Most of us consider whether or not we're someone's partner, parent, child, or friend to be important to who we are. But we also have a lot of ideas about what it means to be a good partner, to be a good parent, or to be a good friend. That's because those statuses of partner, parent, or friend comprise specific identities that contain both shared and individual ideas.

You may be catching onto a theme here. Like our ideas about how we see ourselves, how we understand our relational roles also come from messages that we hear throughout our life. The ones we buy into, that are repeated, shared by those we value, and prove useful in our own experiences, form memorable messages that actually influence how we see ourselves in those specific roles. To illustrate, Angela shares an example:

One of my identities is that of a stepparent. When my partner and I married in 1995, his three children from his first marriage were young (five, seven, and eight years old). While I'd never been married before my husband, I was somewhat comfortable and familiar with the role I'd be stepping into. I was the product of a family with a stepfather. While our upbringing wasn't always perfect—my stepdad could be a terse and closed communicator—I watched my mother negotiate our spaces and manage her emotions when we had interactions with my stepdad and my biological dad. She was what I'd call a "smooth operator" when it came to communication and deescalating the woes and frustrations of her former and current partner as it related to us children. I believe because of this, when I was planning to marry, she and I had a few conversations on this topic.

She let me know from her experiences that it would be important to make sure that the channels of communication were clear and open with my partner and respectful with his ex-wife. She let me know there would be inevitable tensions ... we were human after all. However, this was what I'd need to negotiate if I were to thrive personally and relationally. She did not withhold the hard side of this, letting me know that complicated and difficult challenges would inevitably arise, but that with honesty and transparency I could be of sound mind. While there was not one specific memorable message, I recall a series of memorable conversations with my mom that helped me find calm within this new relationship dynamic. Most importantly, these memorable conversations helped me find peace of mind in communicating with my partner, the children, and even his ex-wife. The memorable messages attached to these conversations formed my sense of what it meant to be a successful stepparent, someone who can navigate the spaces in between.

As with this example, where Angela came to understand what being a stepparent meant from both observations of her own stepparent and explicit communication with her mother over time, we learn what it means to occupy a relational role through both ambient messages (via observation or experience) and direct messages (someone telling us). We receive messages like this about all of the many relational roles we occupy, and gauge our successes or failures in living up to those roles by comparing our own behavior to the scripts generated from those messages.

Our relational roles are important to many of us, but we also identify with (or are identified by others to) the larger social and cultural groups to which we belong. Gender, racial, religious, sexual, and other larger cultural identities do shape our social experience in many ways. We receive an abundance of messages repeated by many sources that explain the expectations and norms surrounding our various cultural groups. Some of these can validate and inspire us, and sometimes they draw from stereotypes or discriminatory messages that discourage and harm.

This can even intersect in a compilation of identities. For instance, Angela typically recognizes the ways she must negotiate different spaces and expectations as they pertain to how society views her as a Black woman. Often, interactions with others make her simultaneously aware that her race, gender, and age are at play in the situation. But context matters. She recalls one of the first times she traveled outside of the United States. The realization that her race was not a part of the equation—something that she typically had to negotiate—created a palpable memorable experience. The freedom of being in a culture and country where her identity as a Black woman was not a part of the negotiation of space, experiencing a society where the norm was that Black and Brown people held professional careers or had their own businesses, was at first a shock but then an affirmation. The simplicity of finding a Black barbershop to get a haircut or finding local merchandise that catered to her skincare or clothing wishes was grounding. The way identity is made visible or invisible can prompt memorable messages for many of us.

For a recent example,[15] a team of researchers looked at how parents of Black daughters negotiated their own memorable messages about Black womanhood with the messages they wanted to pass onto their daughters—sometimes the same, and sometimes intentionally different. That is, the study considered how parents' memorable messages that they received influenced the messages they wanted to intentionally pass down to their children—what they wanted to tell their daughters about what it meant to be a Black woman. One of the most common findings from their study regarded the parents' own messages about Black hair. Specifically, they wanted to counter any of their own messages they received based in racist beauty standards or even standards of hair within Black communities that they thought would hurt their children's self-esteem, and ensure instead that they passed on messages to their children that emphasized that their hair was beautiful. An additional finding discussed the way parents of Black children intentionally crafted memorable messages to anticipate social needs—serving the anticipatory socialization function of memorable messages. Specifically, they wanted to counter negative messages they thought their children might experience or have to deal with throughout their lives, or even that they themselves might encounter about how they wanted to raise their children within their families and communities.

An especially meaningful finding from this study demonstrates what the researchers called the *dynamic nature of memorable messages.*[16] Most memorable message research, our own included, and even in the broader sense most research on identity-socialization, focuses on *anticipatory* socialization—preparing us ahead of time for what we might encounter in the world or what we should do under different circumstances in the real or hypothetical future. Many memorable messages are those we receive when we're much younger about a circumstance that may or may not occur down the line. This study also found examples of *reactive socialization,* or when someone communicates or sends a message in response to a specific situation that is actively occurring. For example, a family member of a Black child commenting on their hair, and the parent intercepting with a specific comment about accepting the child's hair or reinforcing their beauty and self-worth. Memorable messages about identities may be both anticipatory and reactive—providing insights about what identity can or should look like before we encounter various situations or after we do.

All of us occupy many social identities, as we do personal and relational identities. We receive both anticipatory and reactive messages that instruct us on how to best embody those identities, or sometimes how to protect ourselves on the basis of them. But those identities also intersect, interrelate, and influence one another. Our experiences within and among those identities vary in terms of power and context.[17] Memorable messages occur within such contexts. While these messages tend to be interpersonal, and delivered between or among individuals, they exist in the context of culture.

Memorable messages involving identity-relevant content help socialize us into our various social roles. In part, this occurs through the process of identity anchors and scripts.

Identity Anchors and Scripts

Researchers describe scripts as mental frameworks that guide our expectations and behavior during a variety of social interactions.[18] Scripts are the working mental models we have for what we should do and think when we're doing something with other people. You have scripts for basically everything you do, or anytime you do, think, or feel something that you aren't really critically thinking about—it's probably guided by your cognitive script for that thing. For example, when you are entering a space as someone else is leaving it, you probably, without really thinking about it, hold the door for the person. They may, without really thinking about it, say "Thanks" and you likely respond with "No problem" or "You're welcome." This common experience is an example of a script—a model that our minds have for how we should act, what we should do, how we should feel, or what we should think under different circumstances that we encounter throughout our lives.

Because memorable messages often socialize us into understanding our core value system and defining our roles as individuals, as members of families or other social relationships, and as members of the various cultural groups to which we belong, they can form identity scripts that tell us what a person who occupies a given role ought to do within that role.

Take for example the identity scripts of "mother." The scripts associated with motherhood form a template for how we expect mothers to act. For those of us who have mothers, this means we evaluate the behaviors of our mothers against those scripts. For those who are mothers, that script informs how they behave within the role of mother, or how they compare their behavior as a mother. For example, a woman likely has her own script for "mother" based on a combination of her relationship with her own mother and common cultural depictions of motherhood in television, media, and through her other social circles. If she then becomes a mother, her identity script for "mother" is going to be formed from many sources, but a prominent source is the memorable messages she received, directly or indirectly, about motherhood.[19,20] That might include observations from her own mother, her positive and negative experiences with mothers in her life, meaningful advice that friends and family gave her, or common wisdom about mothers or motherhood depicted in cultural narratives. If she had a tense or troubled relationship with her mother, it might include significant deviations from her own upbringing.

Taken together, we can consider how identity scripts form at the intersection of our personal, social, and relational identities. For a different example, take the role of "sibling" and consider variations based on age, gender, birth order, culture, or even the varied personalities of siblings. The identity script for "sibling" that one holds factors in these and many other concepts and experiences.

Think about your own identity scripts. What are the important roles you occupy in your own life? These might be relational (who are you in relation to other people—child, parent, sibling, friend, partner, etc.). They may be occupational or organizational (your job, education, or clubs you belong to or memberships you hold).

Now, think about what memorable messages helped inform your ideas about that role.

- What are the characteristics of your identity script?
- Where did they come from?
- What memorable messages informed those ideas?

A lot of recent research[21,22] has delved into the concept of memorable messages as identity anchors, especially in the context of resilience. As we have mentioned a few times in describing the basic purposes of memorable messages, these messages offer us guidance, comfort, or wisdom during moments of stress, uncertainty, and transition throughout our life. For example, we might have received a number of memorable messages that lead us to value kindness. Through the many roles we occupy and many experiences we have, that anchor of "I am a kind person" may stabilize our sense of self.

Another way of thinking about this function is to consider that the values of these messages anchor our sense of identity or self-concept during times of instability. When the earth moves beneath our feet during a crisis or major life transition, the memorable messages that shape our self-concept and identity also stabilize it, keeping it steady in moments of change. So, if we are in a disagreement with a friend, or managing tension at work, or dealing with a breakup, a major move, or anything else that leads us to feel uncertain, having those identity anchors that make us feel like a consistent person within our own value system helps to steady our self-concept.

This is part of what lets us feel a sense of stability even amid significant changes in our life.

Let's pause to reflect. What are your identity anchors? What grounds your sense of yourself? What memorable messages did you receive that led you to those anchors?

Now that you have had space to reflect on your overall self-concept, your role-based identity scripts, and your more personal identity anchors, reflect overall on how the memorable messages you have received affect how you see yourself.

- How do memorable messages inform your self-concept?
- How do your identity anchors and scripts and their associated memorable messages affect how you see yourself overall?
- Are you satisfied with the messages you received that influenced how you see yourself?

7

Behavioral Impact and Self-Assessment

During one of our research studies, a participant who we'll call Amelia shared an unfortunately common story with us. Seeking input from her doctor on troubling and disruptive symptoms related to perimenopause, Amelia recalled her doctor telling her that the symptoms she reported lived primarily in her head. She vividly remembered the memorable message from her doctor: "You're overexaggerating." The message left her feeling dismissed and discouraged. Perhaps most importantly, she reported that this message stopped her from asking for help from other healthcare providers.

To us, Amelia reported that her doctor's discouraging memorable message left her with a new hesitancy about talking to *any* doctor. She felt unsure of the experience of her own symptoms in her body because a medical provider had told her that they weren't real. Of course, there are many emotional and psychological consequences to messages like that, but for Amelia, a really important one was that it affected her behavior. She didn't go back to the doctor for *years*.

As we conclude the section of this book exploring the basic features and impact of memorable messages, we discuss in this chapter the ways that memorable messages help us decide what to do, and help us evaluate or make sense of our behavior after the fact. Throughout this discussion, we encourage you to consider how your own memorable messages inform the choices you make and the actions you take.

We also want to be clear here that while memorable messages certainly do inform and affect our decision-making processes, they don't *have* to. So far in this book, we have mostly explored memorable messages from the perspective of the recipient—looking back on the messages we have received and how they ultimately influenced us. But many messages influence us in ways that are bound to be unproductive, even harmful. We don't have to remain affected or remain influenced by every message we receive. In this chapter we'll discuss the research on how memorable messages affect behavior, but in the next few chapters, we will shift our discussion toward what to do if you don't like how your memorable messages impact your own behavior.

Memorable Messages as Scripts for Behavior

Recall that memorable messages inform our identity scripts. They form frameworks in our mind for how we see ourselves. For example, you may have received memorable messages about work ethic, instructing you to work hard and try your best. As a result, those messages may have resulted in an identity script in which you see yourself as someone who is hardworking.

Similarly, memorable messages build frameworks for how we ought to behave in a variety of situations. That same message, "Work hard and try your best," may also form a *behavioral script* for work-related behavior. A behavioral script, like an identity script, is a mental framework. Whereas identity scripts describe the traits a certain type of person might exhibit, behavioral scripts instruct us about how we should behave in different situations. For example, we might have a behavioral script about work ethic that tells us we should always try our hardest, or give it our all. We might have a behavioral script about helping people that tells us we should always make time for others. Or we may have a behavioral script about relationships that tells us we should be honest or attentive or romantic.

Importantly, while we receive many messages that may result in behavioral scripts, we do not and cannot always equally enact them. For instance, although most of us who grew up in the U.S. likely received an abundance of messages about work ethic, some of which probably did become memorable due to repetition, utilization, or because someone meaningful shared them with us, certainly not every single person is able to try their hardest at everything. "Trying their hardest" might look different from person to person based on life circumstances and ability. Later in this chapter we'll explore how behavioral memorable messages also present comparison points for self-assessment of the behaviors we do enact, even when they deviate from the ideals of the messages we receive, and why we sometimes reject those messages altogether.

We receive many messages that result in behavioral scripts throughout our life. This is especially true of formative messages we receive when we're young, such as those that tell us how to behave in social situations ("Hold the door," "Always say thank you"), but memorable messages, like the one Amelia received, can influence our behavioral scripts at any point in the lifespan.

During a moment of stress and vulnerability, experiencing disruptive changes in her body, Amelia shared her concerns with a doctor. Her choice to consult a doctor in the first place likely stemmed from other memorable messages she received throughout her life (for instance, "If something feels off in your body, you should ask a doctor about it"). At her appointment, her doctor dismissed her experiences and brushed off her concerns. As a result, she left with a new set of behavior-oriented memorable messages that replaced her initial instinct to consult with a doctor when something felt off in her body. Now, Amelia feels that doctors will not take her concerns seriously, and will make her feel bad. Her new behavioral script for her health encourages her to keep her feelings to herself. For Amelia, this meant that it took a few years before she sought the advice of a healthcare provider again. For many, this means they might delay care when it's needed, or second-guess themselves when it comes to how they're feeling or if something is wrong.

We can think about behavioral scripts as somewhat formulaic. If X happens, then we do Y. For instance, if you're feeling sick, then you go to a doctor. Or, if you're not feeling well, then it might be in your head and doctors won't take you seriously, so you shouldn't say anything. These are very different behavioral scripts for the same experience. We learn the "Y" in our behavioral scripts in part from the memorable messages we receive. In Amelia's case, at an important moment, a person who could have responded with empathy and compassion instead responded with dismissal.

In other circumstances, we might encounter a response that validates and encourages our initial behavior, reinforcing the earlier behavioral script. For instance, if you have a script that tells you to go to a doctor when you're sick, and your experiences with doctors are, unlike Amelia, relatively positive, that script is reinforced with every one of those experiences. Every time a doctor takes your complaints seriously or is able to resolve a concern, that initial message and its initial script feel more and more valid and true. But if you encounter a doctor who makes you feel bad for seeking out care, then the script might be challenged.

For the types of memorable messages we receive when we're young, which tell us how we ought to behave when meeting new people, starting a new job, when we get sick or get a flat tire or start a new relationship or anything else, the more those messages are reinforced by the life experiences we have, and the more they continue to guide our future behaviors. Take for instance a common memorable message: "Don't underestimate the power of first impressions." You have likely received a similar message yourself. If so, you might find those messages validated—with first encounters with new people significantly forming your opinions of them, and their opinions of you. Each time you find that message to be true, it becomes more solidly ingrained as a template for your future behavior, reminding you to be extra mindful during your initial interactions with new people.

Alternatively, when something undermines those messages, the scripts become less stable or may shift altogether. Consider a common childhood memorable message as an example: "Treat other people the way you want to be treated." The golden rule message that many of us heard as children includes a prescription for a behavioral script—that is, it tells us what we should do. When interacting with people, treat them as you would want to be treated. Generally, this is implied to mean with kindness, respect, and empathy. While some of you may still follow the golden rule, most folks have had many experiences where they were not treated the way they wanted to be, and as a result, the behavioral script instilled through that message can become shaky and unstable. When we doubt the validity of those messages, when we no longer endorse it, it becomes less impactful toward our behavior, even if we still remember it.

Self-Concept and Assessing Our Own Behavior

As we discussed in the last chapter, memorable messages inform our self-concepts, or how we see ourselves. How we see ourselves is important in how we think about, assess, or evaluate our own behavior. In the last chapter, we discussed the idea of the self as, in many ways, a reflection of other people—our roles, our relationships, and how others reflect ideas of who we are back to us when we interact with them. But we also sometimes take a mirror to ourselves without really thinking about it, subtly examining our own behavior and how it compares with the ideas we have about ourselves.

Recall again the first two memorable messages we shared with you in this book—Val's familial message "in this family, we help people" and Angela's mother's two "be carefuls." These messages instruct us to think about ourselves as the type of people who help others. When we incorporate these messages into our self-concept, we have a standard against which to evaluate the choices we make in day-to-day life.

About 20 years ago, a team of researchers began to consider if memorable messages impact our behavior. Their research found through several studies[1,2] and replicated in others[3] that memorable messages help form a point through which we assess and compare our behavior. They drew upon a theory called Control Theory's idea of a negative feedback loop, which says that people will watch or monitor their own behavior, and sometimes make adjustments if the outcome of their behavior doesn't quite match up with their goal or standard. In simpler terms, that means memorable messages influence us by helping establish how we see ourselves. Then, we compare our actual behavior to that vision of ourselves.

For example, say someone really took to heart the memorable messages they received about kindness—"Treat others with kindness" or "Always be kind." If we internalize those messages, we can develop that as a sort of standard for how we think we should behave. Then, when that someone has a standard of being a kind person, and they make a comment that clearly hurts someone's feelings, they may go back and determine that their behavior (making a mean comment) didn't align with their standard (being kind), and make an adjustment (apologizing).

In the case of our own messages about helping others, our standard (helpful) becomes a comparison point for our actions. When Angela stopped to offer a stranger a ride, she evaluated her behavior positively because it aligned with her self-concept as a helpful person. But if she had engaged in a behavior that she might assess as not so helpful, she would have been likely to make some kind of adjustment or just not feel great about her choice.

Research[4] has found that memorable messages help form the goals or standards to which we compare the outcomes of our behavior. For instance, if we received a memorable message like "Don't be a quitter," that message can form a reference point that we compare our actions and outcomes against. When someone who received that kind of message encounters challenging situations, the behind-the-scenes of their decision-making takes a few things into account:

1. The *reference value* that forms the standard they're setting for their behavior (don't be a quitter). This is where memorable messages factor in. When we recall and internalize behaviorally oriented memorable messages, many of them being prescriptive formulas that socialize us to behave in particular ways ("Don't be a quitter"; "Always be kind"; "It's important to try your best"), we incorporate them into our sense of self as we discussed in the last chapter. When we do this, they become that reference value—a standard, ideal, or goal for how we see ourselves. For a message like "Don't be a quitter," that means we would see ourselves as someone who doesn't quit, and that becomes the point to which we compare the behaviors we actually engage in.

2. Next, the process of assessing and adapting our behavior takes into account how someone perceives their own behavior in the situation. This is basically a reflection of how someone is managing or coping with a situation. For instance, when faced with a challenging situation, someone might endure it with difficulty, or they may choose to leave. If an individual is struggling with a new expectation at work, they may try to power through, adapt, and work harder (endure it, but with difficulty), or they may give up and not complete the new expectation or just quit (leave).

3. After someone perceives their own behavior, they make a comparison between their perception of their behavior, and the reference value they set for themselves. For example, if they are

working through the challenging situation and enduring it, they may feel they are living up to the standard (i.e., not a quitter). If they feel like they want to change paths or directions, they may feel they are not living up to the standard learned through their memorable messages.

4. Lastly, the negative feedback process occurs. This is an academic way of saying we either experience some kind of discrepancy in step 3, or we don't. In the scenario where we feel we're living up to the message—sticking it out, we aren't experiencing any negative feedback, and no adjustment or behavior change needs to be made. But if the challenging situation leads to someone engaging in a behavior that might fall under the umbrella of "quitting," they may experience negative feedback because there is a discrepancy between how they perceive themselves (their self-concept, informed by that memorable message) and how they perceive their behavior (what they actually do in a situation).

If the last step there results in negative feedback—that is, a person feels like there is a big discrepancy between how they see themselves and what they're actually doing, they're likely to make some kind of adjustment. In this example, that adjustment might be remaining in a situation they would otherwise benefit from leaving because they don't want to see themselves as a quitter. Alternatively, it might mean minimizing their emotional response, for example by trying to appear that they are toughing it out to others. Or it might mean experiencing guilt and distress over their ultimate decision.

A desire to reduce the experience of dissonance motivates us to make these adjustments, either psychologically or behaviorally, in how we think, express ourselves, or ultimately behave. Cognitive dissonance occurs when something doesn't quite match up in our minds—when we hold two or more ideas, thoughts, or engage in behaviors that demonstrate some kind of inconsistency.[5] That is, if how we see ourselves is different from how someone else seems to be seeing us, or different from how we behave, or if we hold onto two ideas that seem to contradict one another—all of those can prompt cognitive dissonance. For example, if you think of yourself as an environmentally conscious person, then accidentally drop some trash on the ground when you meant to toss it into the trash can. If you leave it on the ground, you're likely to experience some dissonance, because your self-concept (environmentally conscious person) is not aligned with your actions (someone who is littering). Dissonance is psychologically uncomfortable, and we usually feel some motivation to reduce it or get rid of it completely when it occurs.

The memorable messages we receive that shape our core ideas about who we are, and how we ought to behave, construct the foundation that we compare our actions against. Thus, when our actions or sometimes the actions of others suggest that we are not living up to our own self-image, then we experience that dissonance. Minimally, dissonance is uncomfortable, but memorable message research on behavioral self-assessment suggests that for many of us, we will take actions in order to reduce it and align our behavior more closely with our memorable message.

Importantly, these processes don't always play out consciously through our active, intentional thinking. While we do sometimes think through our decisions and actively compare them to our ideals, we often do all of this behind the scenes—when our brains kind of guide us through the day on autopilot. As we move into the next few chapters, we want to remind readers that just because we have a tendency to let these scripts guide us mindlessly doesn't mean we have to continue doing that. When you become aware of the scripts that guide your actions, you can exert some control over them.

Message Valence and Behavior

A memorable message's valence also affects our behavior. Message valence, which just means how positive or negative we feel a particular memorable message is, strongly influences how we ultimately feel about the message, and what we ultimately do with it. A lot of memorable message research finds message valence associated with the kind of relationship we have with the message source (the person who sent us the message—how positive or negative we feel about that relationship overall),[6] likelihood to engage in a variety of behaviors (like helping someone, seeking assistance for ourselves, or health behaviors), and even personal outcomes like self-esteem[7] or self-efficacy. In the context of behavior, we want to dive a little deeper into a specific research study about memorable messages and aging.

Patricia Gettings and Kai Kuang recently looked at the role of memorable messages in the process of communication about aging.[8]

Guided by a perspective that argues individuals have some agency in their own aging experience through their communication, Gettings and Kuang considered memorable messages as a specific unit of communication—focused on messages that contained content about aging ("You're as old as you feel," "Growing older is not fun," or "As you grow older you grow more patient").[9]

Specifically, they considered how the content of memorable messages (what the message was saying) and the valence (how positive or negative those messages were) related to the message recipient's behavioral choices to seek relevant information about aging and whether or not they felt like they could handle aging. Social scientists call that coping efficacy—feeling like one is capable of coping with a situation. Their findings suggest that more positive memorable messages about aging left older adults feeling more capable of handling aging, and more likely to plan to seek out meaningful information about aging.

We point to this study for a few reasons. First, the three examples, which are data points from that particular study, of aging-related memorable messages actually do not all follow the prescriptive formula we described earlier. Instead, they contain general ideas about aging. Even still, these messages influenced people's behavior and emotional state in meaningful ways. Second, aging is an important part of life—if we're lucky, all of us eventually move into the social group of older adults. Understanding the types of messages that contribute to more effective relationships with aging and healthier aging-related behavior is an important idea. Third, this study really underscores the simple but powerful idea of message valence. Often the exact content of a message is less important than feeling like the message carries a positive sentiment, or positive intent toward the receiver. It's such a simple idea, but has so much influence on the way we live our lives and what we ultimately do with the messages we internalize.

Internalized Messages as Motivation or Discouragement

Part of what makes memorable messages memorable as opposed to the many other messages that don't stick with us over time is that we *internalize* them. Internalization is the product of what we discussed in the last chapter. When those messages start to become a part of how we see ourselves, how we believe we should behave, and how we evaluate the behavior of ourselves and others, we have internalized the message. It becomes a part of us.

Internalized messages, as with all messages, can be positive or negative. When we internalize messages that help us cope with difficult or challenging situations, they can build resilience.[10] For instance, memorable messages that validate a person's capabilities like "You are strong," "You are capable," and "Your family always believes in you"—if we buy them, they can encourage or motivate us toward resilience. These messages are especially helpful to individuals who pair them with self-compassion.[11]

Alternatively, messages that might seem to encourage resilience like "Don't be a quitter" or "Tough it out," when absent of more compassionate contexts, can have the opposite effect. As life situations challenge us, people who endorse those messages might feel the need to suffer in silence, minimize their emotional response by holding back from those they love, or remain in jobs, relationships, or situations that otherwise don't serve them. Instead, these messages prompt that dissonance response we talked about earlier and make us feel worse rather than better.[12]

We also internalize messages that are directed to us not as individuals, but as members of the various social groups to which we belong. For example, messages about race, gender, sexuality, age, religion, socioeconomic status, and even region can carry ideas that affect how we see ourselves and how we ought to behave. There are also behavioral consequences for internalizing stigmatized messages, or messages that encourage us to believe parts of our identity are different in ways that are bad, or the outcomes of behaviors related to our group memberships. Earlier, Val shared an example of this in relation to her coming-out stories. But there are many social groups to which we belong that influence our ideas about ourselves and the choices we make.

A lot of our own research focuses on the memorable messages that women receive during early adolescence. One of our studies looked at the messages girls received about menstruation—or really, the lack of clear communication in many cases.[13] The participants in this study highlighted messages that told them to be ashamed of their bodies, positioned menstruation as dirty and gross and something to hide from their brothers or fathers, or just left them confused and uncertain. (We named that study "I thought I was dying" because that was such a common memorable message theme those participants reported experiencing at their first period.) In the case of that study and that context, the stigmatized messages that girls received about menstruation left them feeling uncertain, downplaying their health-related concerns when talking to their parents or pediatricians, and in some cases remaining with them into adulthood and affecting their relationships with their bodies over time.

For the women in that study, many left with a behavioral script that their period was not something they should talk to anyone about. Scripts like that, and experiences like Amelia's, work together to form expectations about how certain subjects will be received by others. Our expectations about how other people will react to us, be it our friends, family, or doctors, inform the choice we make as communicators. In this way, our memorable messages can leave us with lasting, often lifelong influences on our behavioral choices.

Memorable messages, good or bad, can motivate us to take specific actions or engage in specific behaviors. Take for example a brief reflection from Angela on how she came to become involved in this research:

I believe one of the reasons I'm so drawn to the sexual health aspects of how memorable messages impact use over our lifespan is because my household was one where conversations about sex and sexual health were pretty open and common. Even though this was not uncommon in my own home, I realized unexpectedly when having a conversation with my very Christian friends in my religious high school that this wasn't the norm in other folks' homes. Even as an adult, conversations about sex and sexual health with my nieces and nephews are typical. They laugh sometimes and occasionally roll their eyes, however they will often sit and listen to my inquiry about their sex lives with their respective partners. They are also comfortable asking me questions about most sexual health topics. I believe that the ease with which we talked about difficult topics has impacted me and my family members. This doesn't mean we are all comfortable but it does mean that we all have expectations that these sorts of private conversations will be had. I feel this motivates and encourages us as a family to be candid about what happens in private.

Above, Angela offers an example of an ambient memorable message. Talking about sometimes taboo topics openly within her family became a memorable idea over time. Upon realizing that her household was the exception rather than the rule, she became interested in studying why certain topics are private. This memorable message motivated her behavior—prompting a research agenda that she has spent two decades of her professional life investigating.

Memorable messages affect our behavior in many ways—big and small. By guiding the ideals that form our self-concept, how we see ourselves, we incorporate them into the big choices we make in life—like what we want to do with it, how we want to spend our time, what career we might want to pursue, how we spend our money, the political actions we choose to take, and the types of people we might be drawn to. But they also guide our choices in many small ways and through many daily actions. Whether or not we take the time to be polite, empathetic, or supportive, what we expect from communication with others, whether or not we stick with something or change directions, how compassionate we might be with ourselves or those in our lives, and even whether or not we decide to clean something today or tomorrow, may all be informed by ideas we internalize through the memorable messages we receive in our life.

Our big life choices often reflect the many little ones we make day to day, so attending to what guides us to make those decisions, and whether or not we're happy with them, is a worthwhile exercise. In the last chapter, we encouraged you to reflect on how the memorable messages you received affected your self-concept or how you see yourself. We encourage you here to continue that reflection:

- In what ways does your self-concept inform the choices you make?
- How does it inform how you feel about those choices?
- In what ways do memorable messages impact your behavior or how you feel about your behavior?

In essence, we suggest thinking deeply about what messages you have internalized. Do those messages motivate or discourage you?

Try to think about two to three specific memorable messages that inform your self-concept (it's okay to reuse the messages from the last chapter). Now, consider how those messages make you feel about the choices you have made, or make, in your life.

Some messages obviously harm or obviously help us, but a lot of the messages we receive live somewhere in the middle, or perhaps only become clearly hurtful or clearly helpful in hindsight. In the next chapter, we'll discuss the characteristics of helpful memorable messages, and consider what to do when our memorable messages help us.

8

When Memorable Messages Help Us

Throughout our lives, we receive messages that help and guide us in so many ways. Sometimes, the person who sent us the message—people like our parents, friends, partners, mentors, or colleagues—intended their words or actions to assist us. Other times, we found comfort, instruction, or utility in those messages completely by accident. Maybe you simply read a line in someone's social media post or felt impacted by a storyline in a television program. Maybe you took a lesson from a friend's story that varied significantly from the point they intended to make. Regardless of intent, many memorable messages can and do serve us in helpful ways throughout our lives. To introduce the concept of helpful memorable messages, Angela will share a brief reflection on one of her own:

"When someone shows you who they are, believe them the first time."

I have always believed that if you pay attention to people, they show you through various actions and behaviors their true nature as an individual. I believe over time, you will see the character of a person, so pay attention. This statement isn't new to our culture. First famously popularized by Maya Angelou, her mentee Oprah Winfrey often repeated it on her daytime talk show. Funnily enough, I once thought the phrase originated with my mother because she'd used it so often, directed toward me and my siblings: "When someone shows you who they are, believe them."

My siblings tell me that I was a perceptive and stealthy child when it came to forming relationships, very cautious of others' intentions, and always asking "Why?" Direct and comfortable with telling adults I didn't want to do something, or that what they said didn't seem wise, I spoke my mind. Despite my perception of my own directness, I have been told by friends on many occasions now, "When I first got to know you, I thought you were aloof." In part, I believe that understanding of me stems from my learned caution toward others. While I had no challenges making friends, I did believe that people show us their true nature, and it isn't always positive and to be trusted.

By contrast, despite also being raised in a household hearing that same message echo in our walls, this wasn't the case for one of my siblings. My sister was quick to friendship and, in turn, quick to experience numerous letdowns from those who didn't serve her. For me, it was second nature, if my young counterparts (acquaintances, neighborhood kids, potential friends) showed me who they were, for me to quickly internally decide whether I could or could not be friends with them. But my sister gave everyone as many chances as they needed.

It's funny, because my mother used to also repeat the popular and somewhat contradictory saying: "don't judge a book by its cover," by which she meant "give people time, Angela." I was not built of that cloth. My older sister however—well she loved everyone ... and I mean everyone. She is one of the kindest people I know. She literally has given the clothes off her back to make sure someone feels happy, comfortable, or safe. I am still very much a stoic, distant, and watchful person before I enter into a relationship with you. My sister, well, she's your best friend right out of the gate. Because of this, she has experienced relationships when folks have shown her themselves and she's struggled to recognize their true intentions.

This message helped guide my philosophy toward the people I want to invest in and become close to, and avoid relationships with people who don't put in the effort or who bear ill will toward me. But the same message would not be helpful to everyone. My sister's openness, though I think it sometimes leads to her getting hurt, is a part of who she is, so that message might not have been helpful to her. She might suggest that writing people off too soon is unhelpful.

Throughout the last few chapters, we've talked about the ways that memorable messages can influence us through our behavior, self-concept, and relationships. The processes through which memorable messages become impactful occurs regardless of whether that outcome is positive or negative. We offered examples that demonstrated some of the positive outcomes of memorable messages: messages that help us build resiliencies; offer hope, comfort, or clarity; messages that shift our perspectives and offer us a stable vision of ourselves in times of uncertainty, and that let us feel closer to the people who matter to us. In contrast, we also followed messages that highlight some of the not-so-positive outcomes—messages that lead us to self-destructive behaviors, leave us feeling alienated or sad, or make us question our self-worth.

In this section of the book, we will guide you through understanding how your own memorable messages have helped or hurt you, and what to do with messages you want to embrace and those you might want to reject. In choosing to lead with the positive, we'll start off with what to do when memorable messages help us. As another example, Val will share a message that helped guide her:

"No one gets anywhere alone."

When thinking about the challenges we encounter throughout our life, I think we sometimes face a temptation to minimize the other characters in our stories. I consider most of my own memorable messages that I have shared so far in this book helpful in one way or another, but when considering memorable messages that have specifically helped me, I recall a sort of silly one.

As much as I have benefited from the wisdom of those in my own life, I also found a helpful message from a line uttered by the television character Leslie Knope, Amy Poehler's hyper-positive and hardworking Parks and Recreation *character: "No one gets anywhere alone."*

That message meant so much to me that I repeated it atop the acknowledgments page of my dissertation. I remind myself of that message whenever I think of my accomplishments, or how I have managed challenges in the past. And I call upon that message today whenever a challenging situation or new difficulty arises.

For example, I recall my time as an undergraduate student, and when I think about the early obstacles I faced in those first days of adulthood, I am tempted to position myself and my own traits—brains or hard work or determination—as the central features that helped overcome personal or professional obstacles. Sometimes, for some of us, it is more helpful to remind ourselves what we're capable of—that our drive or effort or talent led us to success. For me, I find it more helpful to let my mind wander to the countless times I sat with my best friend on her bedroom floor while whatever horror movie she was watching at the time played in the background—venting or crying or gossiping. I think about how many times my head hit her shoulder in tears of frustration or how many times we giggled over a margarita while those same breakups or conflicts or professional hurdles faded into a foggy memory.

Remembering that every win and every loss comes accompanied by a community of love and care helps me feel connected to the people around me, reinforces the value of those relationships, and reminds me to show up for them too. Every word I write comes from a lifetime of connections to others—of the lessons I learned from my mentors and teachers and my own students today, to the interactions with the people in my life who helped shape who I am and support me and my efforts in too many ways to document here. For a self-proclaimed introvert who definitely enjoys my alone time, it's important for me to embrace those connections and focus on the value and meaning they bring to my life.

A related message I take when reflecting on the importance of valuing the people who help us get anywhere also allows me to reframe challenging experiences I have had. While thinking about challenges one must overcome to succeed at anything, per my Leslie Knope reminder, I think about my friends, family, colleagues, spouse—everyone who I've bounced an idea off of or who listened to me vent or who congratulated me when I succeeded or distracted me when I needed to get my mind off of something, who taught me or gave me advice, or helped remind me to be present and remember that I'm more than one thing. Focusing on those who helped makes the actual challenge seem small. I remind myself when thinking of my history to think less about the obstacles and more about who showed up for me during them. As new challenges in life arise, when asking "How will I manage this?" I remind myself to answer "Not alone."

Our cultural negativity bias[1] (we have a tendency to focus more on negative events, communication, and emotions than positive ones) sometimes leads us to devote more attention to the messages we have received that hurt us than those that have helped us. Part of taking ownership of the messages we *want* to use means identifying those that have helped us and actively embracing them. Think deeply about why they help and what we want to get out of them, adapt them as needed, and evoke them routinely to get the most out of those meaningful messages.

Messages can be helpful for a variety of reasons. Maybe they're helpful because they assist in making a particular decision, or help us make sense of an experience. Maybe they make us feel better, or challenge us to make choices that help us grow. For the message Val shared above, the words are helpful because she *finds them* helpful—they help her frame her accomplishments and tougher moments in a way that she finds psychologically comforting and helps facilitate closer connections and appreciation for the people in her life. By contrast, Angela believes that the message she shared at the start of this chapter has helped her to avoid unnecessary relational hardships by offering a healthy caution. Finding a message helpful always falls to our interpretation, meaning that *we* make sense of a message as helpful or not helpful.

Remember—meanings are in people, not in the message itself. The same message that helps one person can hurt another, or one person might find a message uplifting and inspiring while another finds little value in it. Messages are what we make of them. For a person who needs to be more open, messages encouraging caution may backfire. For a person who needs to be more cautious, those messages may be helpful. Val finds it helpful to decenter herself sometimes, and feels comfort in the way others have shown up for her throughout her life. But for someone else, they may need to draw on more internal resiliencies and be reminded of their individual capability. The needs we have, which vary considerably person to person and throughout the lifespan, shape the meaning we take from a memorable message and help dictate whether or not the message actually helps us.

Try to consider some messages in your life that have helped guide you, brought you comfort, answered a question you needed answered in a meaningful way, or otherwise offered support or assistance.

Once you have identified a few messages, consider what makes those specific messages helpful to you. Try to consider all of the reasons they might be helpful, as completely as possible. Take up as much space as you need here. If you're writing in a physical copy of this book, feel encouraged to use the margins. If you're writing in a journal or elsewhere, use as much space as needed.

How Do I Know If a Message Helped or Hurt Me?

In Chapter 3, we discussed one of the reasons we remember particular messages: because they're useful to us. Importantly, utility refers, in that context, to whether or not we literally *use* them in some way. It doesn't mean we use them in a way that necessarily reflects the best choice for us, or in a way that is good for us, or makes us feel good. It just means we use them. So far, we have positioned the idea of memorable messages as helpful or unhelpful as somewhat of a binary—as if there are two options. But in practice, communication and its outcomes are messy, and how a message serves us can and does vary in many ways.

Some messages and their subsequent outcomes are obvious. They carry overtly positive or negative intent, that inspires and warms or harms and chills us. In reality, many messages and how they affect us are more subtle. Even messages that may help us in some situations, can hurt us in others. Someone encouraged by altruism, by helping people, might end up overly self-sacrificing or not prioritizing themselves, leading to resentment. Someone whose messages built resilience might feel overly self-reliant and not ask for help when needed. Conversely, someone else might need the reminder to think of others, or the encouragement that they can do it on their own. That's why we are taking this chapter to think critically about the messages that help us, how they help us, and how we can get the most out of them.

One way to consider, as a baseline, whether or not a message you received actually helped you is to think about those important moments in life when we would draw upon our memorable messages: times where advice, insights, or comfort help orient and stabilize us, like when we go through major transitions in life such as graduations, new jobs, new relationships, breakups, losses, major conflicts, parenthood, or big moves. Did the message you thought of in those situations do just that? Or did you struggle to identify a message? Perhaps in some situations, you easily recall the memorable message that guides you, and in others, you recall a less helpful one, or no message at all.

Absent messages describe the messages that we wish we would have received during those important moments in life. For instance, in some of our research about menstruation, adult women reflected on the absence of meaningful emotionally or practically supportive messages they received when they first got their period,[2] a finding replicated by other research since.[3] In most of our research studies, we ask participants who recall less helpful messages to tell us what messages they wish they had received instead. We have asked this question in a few research contexts, many major bodily transitions, from menstruation to menopause, but we also consider it in relational contexts—the first time someone has sex, their first major relationship, their first big fight or breakup.

In all of these contexts, and others explored by other research teams, we have found that most people can identify what they think would have been helpful after the fact. Or, even if they don't know exactly what they believe would have been helpful, they know *who* they wanted to hear it from. Absent messages can help identify areas when we didn't receive the kind of support that we needed—those big moments in life where we hope particular people will show up for us and do or say the right thing. When that doesn't happen, that absence of a message can be memorable too.

To consider your own absent messages, and where your helpful messages occurred, we will ask you to consider your life trajectory from as early as you remember to this very moment. What were the big moments in your life that led you to where you are now? There is no right or wrong answer to this question, but consider anything that occurred that contributed to or changed the trajectory of your life from your early childhood through today.

Researchers often call these "turning points,"[4] which are just the big moments in a life or a relationship that shift (or sometimes reinforce) the direction we're moving. Possible examples might be health or development-related moments, like puberty, a major health experience like the diagnosis or treatment of an illness, relational moments like a first partner, a serious relationship, falling in or out of love, moving in with a partner, getting married, breakups or divorces, becoming a parent, making a new friend, professional and academic moments like a really difficult class, an exciting career opportunity, earning a degree, a first big job, promotion or professional challenge, or any other big moment in life. Our life is made up of way too many big (and little) moments to reasonably document here, but as an exercise to get started, try to think of 5–10 of your own big turning points in life. What are 5–10 significant experiences you have had that shaped who you are today? Document these in any way that you find meaningful—writing as much or as little as you want.

For each turning point you identified, did you receive or call upon a memorable message in that moment? For example, earlier, Val shared a story of recalling a friend's advice, "You're exactly where you need to be right now," when transitioning between graduate schools. If you remember it, write the message (or messages, if you recalled more than one) next to the turning point. If you don't remember drawing upon any message, put a little * next to it; we'll come back to those in a moment.

For the messages you do remember, how do you think they impacted your behavior, self-concept, or relationships? Choose one or two, and detail the influence as much as you can. For example, the advice Val's friend shared with her offered her comfort in the moment and reassured her about her own decisions, increasing her confidence. It also benefited the relationship itself, leading to a closer connection to a friend who showed up in a needed moment. Val still considers this message in times of stress, and delivers it to others. Now, think about your own messages and what you did with them.

After you have jotted some of this down, reflect on whether or not you feel that the outcome of the message ultimately helped you in any way, big or small:

- Did it influence your behavior in a way that helped you meet your goals of the moment or in the long term?
- Did it offer you comfort or guidance?
- Did it lead to a positive sense of yourself and your identity?
- Did it make you feel closer to the person who delivered it?

If the answer to one or more of these is "yes," then you can probably say confidently that the message helped you at least a little bit. Alternatively, if the message influenced your behavior in a way you are unsure about (or definitely would have done differently in retrospect), made you feel badly about yourself, or left you feeling let down or unsure about the relationship with the person who sent it to you, then it probably wasn't so helpful. Save those messages for the next chapter.

For the items you put a * next to, here is where the absent messages come into play. Consider that moment, now with the benefit of hindsight:

- What message would you have liked to hear then?
- What message would have been helpful to you?
- From whom would you have liked to hear it?
- How do you think it would have influenced you?

The messages you wrote for yourself are examples of your absent messages—ones you didn't receive, but would have found helpful during those important moments in life. Absent messages often reflect messages we received at a different point in time that we wish we had heard sooner. These absent messages, while representing moments where a message did not help us, are informative in their own way. They help us to make sense of our past experience and understand our learning and growth over time. They can also assist us in identifying memorable messages we may still be hanging onto that have outlived their usefulness.

Now, it's important to distinguish between helpful messages and positive messages, even though so far in this chapter we've mostly described messages that we would describe as both. In the last chapter, we discussed the value of positive messages. After all, message valence is such a significant factor in how we interpret memorable messages and how they impact important things like our self-esteem or feeling like we're capable of doing something. More positive messages also tend to reflect more positive relationships overall, so that positivity isn't insignificant. More positive messages are often helpful.

Although they can go together, not all helpful messages are positive. We can find help in messages that usefully warn or protect us, even if they may not be particularly upbeat. The example Angela opened this chapter with may not reflect a positive message in a traditional sense, so much as a warning about people's character. But she found the message helpful to how she navigated her own relationships. Neither of us would characterize our mothers' accounts of domestic abuse as positive, but we do describe them as helpful. Recalling examples of the kind of relational treatment we should consider unacceptable throughout our lives (and that we could help others identify as harmful) actively helped us both at different points, even though no reasonable person would characterize those stories as positive. Sometimes messages of tough love legitimately offered what we needed at a particular point, or helped shape our life trajectory toward our desired goals. Maybe a message helped us make a difficult choice, leave a relationship, or find a new job when difficult changes were needed.

We often find growth in discomfort. Memorable messages can sometimes offer help by creating necessary, albeit uncomfortable, feelings that prompt development and change. In light of our next discussion, about identifying the helpful messages we receive in our life, this distinction proves especially meaningful. Not every message that helps us will immediately offer warm and fuzzy feelings. Sometimes the most helpful messages leave us feeling challenged.

From these exercises, you should be able to identify many of the helpful messages you have received in your life as well as those that might have been more helpful instead. Now, let's think about how and why those messages helped you. Take some time to chart how those messages have impacted you in as much detail as you can recall, focusing on the ways they impact your behavior (or self-assessment of that behavior), your identity and self-concept, and your relationship with either the person who sent the message or other people. When engaged in this reflection, be as specific as possible. Again, we encourage you to use as much space as you need. Mark up the margins of this book if you're reading a physical copy or write additional thoughts in a journal or notebook. Avoid censoring your thoughts here or trying to write concisely—let it all out and get it on the page.

Focusing on the helpful messages can elicit feelings of gratitude, which in and of itself is a positive experience. But beyond that, they can help identify the common characteristics of helpful messages and the processes through which they help us. Looking at your messages here that were most helpful to you, do they have anything in common? Content, form, the person they came from, the context you heard it in, what the ultimate impact was? Take some space to reflect on that here. Consider listing these as bullet points or quick notes—what words come to mind that characterize your most helpful memorable messages?

Try to distill a few key traits of helpful memorable messages. In other words, in one sentence, what makes a helpful memorable message for you? Here, try to limit yourself to one sentence (or two at the most).

With this in mind, consider the memorable messages you have received and documented throughout this book. Start identifying which messages helped you and which did not. Give yourself some time to backtrack through the exercises you have already completed. Note in the margins or next to where you wrote your messages whether or not those interactions helped you, using the same process above. Did they help you? How did they help you? What traits do the messages that help you have in common?

When messages help us, they can shift our perspective, give us new insights, develop positive traits, or lend us comfort or reassurance. In some cases, these messages inspire choices that we're proud of or that lead us in the direction we ultimately want to move in. Once you recognize the characteristics of messages that have helped you, you can start to identify them more readily, sometimes even in the moment of receipt.

We also want to recommend that if through this analysis you notice that a lot of your helpful messages have come from the same sources—tell them. Not everyone will have this outcome, but for some of us, we find that a lot of our most helpful messages came from a particular friend, parent, teacher, sibling, grandparent, or maybe our romantic partner. Self-reflection and assessment are important, but so is expressing when those messages help us to the person who delivered them, even if it's 20 years later.

9

When Memorable Messages Hurt Us

Now, we're going to turn to some of our not-so-helpful messages, and take some space to unpack, process, and disrupt messages that no longer serve us. These messages might actively harm or hurt us, or they just might not be all that useful or important to our lives anymore. We understand this leaves a lot of range—from messages that simply no longer apply to those that cause active and sometimes serious harm. All too often, we hang onto messages and continue to allow them to inform our self-concept, help evaluate our behavior, or affect our relationships even when they have outlived their usefulness (or even when they actively harm us). Sometimes we know we're doing that, but more often than not, we don't really think about it until we think about it. Consider this chapter to be a space to start thinking about what messages continue to hold power over you that maybe shouldn't anymore. To start, Val will share a story about how she shifted her perspective on a compilation of memorable messages she received about her professional life.

"Career = Me" Messages

Like many people, I grew up with a particular vision of what success looked like, and it largely revolved around my career. It wasn't just one message that formed this vision, but the culmination of many memorable messages over time, like "what do you want to do with your life" really asking "what job do you want"; and "what are you going to study in school" really meaning "what career are you training for?" Much of the praise I received growing up related to academic success, writing abilities, and work ethic (in the context of school and paying jobs). My entire young adulthood, save one year of service, went to extensive training to do the job I am doing now. "Career-oriented" most certainly would have described me for my entire life up until a few years ago. I think most people who put much of their identity, time, and even relational life (I met my spouse in grad school) into their vocation or trade feel somewhat similar.

We spend a lot of our waking life working, so wanting to do something that feels fulfilling and of course financially supports us makes all the sense in the world. Up until a few years ago, you could find "career" written at the tippy-top of my metaphorical life priorities list. Then, the pandemic shut the world down. Like many college professors, I went from teaching primarily in person to teaching online. During a time of significant instability in the world, challenges to education amid pandemic life, and our own fears and worries, I realized at this time that I was kind of burnt out.

Before 2020, the memorable messages I received about professional life led me to the conclusion that what you do for a living defines you. Because my career was so central to my identity, most of the time, when given the option, I prioritized it. During 2020, while stuck at home evaluating if I should perhaps reconsider my life priorities, I sought a new activity to fill some of the time I was wasting staring at my phone on the couch or obsessively rechecking my email. Like any reasonable social scientist, I started reading studies on happiness.

Careers have an empirically complicated relationship to happiness. We spend a lot of our waking hours working, so how we spend that time, the decisions we make, the people we're around, the stressors involved, all of that absolutely affects whether or not we're happy. But careers themselves and the big career accomplishments that many of us might romanticize are not a meaningful source of happiness, especially not compared with factors like relational quantity and quality,[1] day-to-day behaviors,[2] and environment[3] (and a series of internal factors like personality[4] and genes,[5] but we're not going to get into that here).

We also tend to overestimate the happiness we'll experience from significant career accomplishments. For instance, I went up for tenure this year (and received it—yay). This is a big moment for professors. Don't get me wrong, I was happy, but honestly, I would describe the experience as more anticlimactic than anything. The happiness I felt was brief, not intense, and fleeting. For a moment that I spent more than a decade of my life working toward, we might expect significant happiness associated with the accomplishment. But research says my reaction is to be expected.[6] *Even the big things in our careers often produce little meaningful differences in our happiness. The ways our careers affect our happiness are much smaller—do we feel like we're doing something meaningful with our life day to day? Do we enjoy our colleagues? Do we like the actual work?*

Obviously, realizing that my life priorities would not lead to happiness did not cause me to abandon my career. Even during Covid, amid the decision to make some changes in how I prioritize my time, Angela and I put out a book and launched a lab. We completed two new research projects and designed several others. I like the work I do, and feel privileged to get to do it. But from my happiness research, I thought it might be time to make some changes in how I live my life to decentralize work from my identity. So I also stopped checking my email after 5:00 p.m. and on weekends. I put firm boundaries on when my workday began and ended, and committed to being more present in my relationships (something that does, empirically, make us happy). I also picked up hobbies, and committed to living my non-working life in ways I found meaningful. I decided I would put the same energy that I put into work into activities that do make people happy. The overwhelming realization of burnout because of the sudden shift in my career made me reexamine many of the memorable messages that I had internalized throughout my life that told me my career would make me happy. I realized that they maybe weren't as helpful as I once thought.

Many of us, and many of our less helpful messages, fall into this category. Messages that encouraged my skills and interests led me to a career I am very passionate about. At the time, I found those messages helpful and encouraging, supportive and validating. But all things in moderation. Too much attention to my work life and too many messages structured around what I now understand to only be a small part of myself was not helpful, and was actually hurting me.

These more ambient messages, which come from the world around us and many sources, can also form memorable messages.

These can be some of the hardest messages to identify and, when necessary, release. We share Val's reflection on career-oriented memorable messages not to suggest that you should decenter your own career, but to highlight that, for Val, centering her identity around her career no longer served her.

Some messages clearly and unambiguously harm us. If someone tells you "you're a failure" or "you aren't good enough," those are harmful messages all around. But for many of us, most of the messages we receive could be helpful for one person and harmful for another. Some people might need a little direction and motivation in life—reminders to prioritize their career or praise related to professional or academic accomplishments might have been wildly helpful and validating. For others, messages suggesting they might need to let go a little more could be more helpful. Many young girls and women received a very different set of messages from Val, ones that assumed their priorities in life would obviously fall toward motherhood and marriage and their own interests or pursuits should be considered temporary by comparison. For some of them, those messages might support a life they find meaningful, and for others, they may have preferred the messages Val received.

Messages can also be helpful at one point, and less helpful at another. Recall earlier we shared Val's memorable message about writing. She considers writing to extend beyond a professional skill (she writes for fun too), but messages Val received about her career are deeply entwined with messages about writing, many of which she still values. As a child, teachers and parents acknowledging Val's skills and abilities, talking to her about her interests, and supporting her professional and academic pursuits *were* helpful. But eventually, those messages stopped being helpful.

We also share this story to explain how most of us come to realize our memorable messages might not be serving us: disruption. For Val, the pandemic prompted such an unsatisfying change in her daily routine that it led her to reexamine the choices she made. For many people, a sudden, severe disruption in the norms of their daily lives inspired dozens of reconsiderations. In this instance, the sudden change in how Val did her job disrupted the messages she had previously received that encouraged her to center her identity around her career. When that identity became destabilized during the early days of Covid, she reconsidered it.

Let's take a different context for another example from Angela.

"Sex before marriage is a sin."

Like most who grew up with "Sex before marriage is a sin" as their primary sexual education, I believe it would have been more impactful to receive this message with greater depth or nuance and less fear. Interestingly, I lived in a home where open talk about relationships and sexual health information was actually shared without much shame or embarrassment. However, from seventh grade through college, I attended religious schools. Both the sheer amount of time I spent in those schools and the need to fit into this space meant my peer group became extremely important and powerful in how I moved through the world. This is often true for adolescents and young people coming to identify with people and ideas outside of their family system. I often felt like I lived in two different universes, one at home and another in Christian school and college. I think back now on how silent I was during this time, especially when I realized that most of my friends were not having the same types of open sexual health conversations that I was in my home. I know now that many people grow up receiving especially punitive, fear-centered, and shame-oriented messages about sex, if any, and very few about the beauty of intimacy, or the importance of knowing your body—what you enjoy, or how to have pleasure in loving relationships.

Messages about sex and marriage from my home lived in a vacuum compared to those I heard in school. The religious school was very clear: bearing children outside of marriage or having sex before you married would be sins. Ideas of purity and restraint were God's will.

These ideas I heard in school clearly did not match with my life in my home. Growing up, among my brother and three sisters, even though they eventually married their babies' parents, two of my siblings were pregnant prior to getting married. Beyond my mother saying she would not be their expected babysitter—she had a life to live and had raised her kids—she taught us about safety, love, and long-term commitment. I saw my family accept the choices and experiences of sex and babies before marriage—they happened, they were realities within my family.

However, the environment I was more responsive to and spent a considerable amount of time in was the Christian schools I attended. They felt safe and I was drawn to the rules, even if at home the tone was very different. Even as an older adult, I am still amazed that my husband of 30 years was my first sexual relationship and that it didn't happen until after we were married.

As I look back at the time of life after college when we first met, I feel that I put so much stress on myself and was led by religious fears and anxieties prior to our marriage and throughout the first few years. I feel unshackled from these ideologies now—I feel there is much more nuance in how we think about sex, sexuality, and sexual health. Most importantly, I believe when people understand their bodies—what is pleasurable and who they are attracted to—with openness and curiosity, that this can be the best beginning to connectivity and longevity and open communication in relationships.

Unhelpful Messages About Sex

Angela's example reflects a lot of common experiences with messages about sex and sexuality. Even though she was raised in a home that encouraged open communication about sex, educational environments are powerful socializers—and her teachers' and peers' convictions about sex before marriage still impacted her. She received many messages that led to feeling stress over ideas of intimacy, which she eventually rejected.

As we've mentioned, most of our own research on memorable messages focuses on messages about sexual behavior, sexuality or sexual orientation, and women's health. We frequently give lectures and presentations and teach classes around the idea of memorable messages, and often share the common messages people receive on these subjects. During these discussions, folks always come up to us after or interject during the talks to express how much they relate to the messages we share—unfortunately, usually the negative ones.

For an example, we will talk through the results from one of our own research studies that investigated the types of memorable messages women recalled about sexual health.[7] In that study, women reported messages that fell under three main categories: protection, danger, and abstinence.

Let's start with abstinence, as many folks can relate to abstinence-only messaging around sexual behavior. Messages that encourage abstinence told participants in that study that only completely avoiding sex would keep them safe, or not to have sex before marriage in most cases. Importantly, while many of these messages focus on abstaining to protect against the physical dangers of sexual activity (like STIs and STDs), many more focus on the emotional dangers of sex (like heartbreak or stigmatization) and that abstinence would protect against that.

Some of these messages shamed participants. For instance, one person from that study noted "the whole unwrapped candy being passed around the class and that abstinence was important" as their memorable message. The idea of giving a future spouse a "used gift" or comparing sexually-active-before-marriage individuals to food that had had many hands on it were common expressions that people recalled and that stuck with them over time. In other studies we've conducted, we heard similar sorts of messages from participants about abstinence:

> *"I remember that the educators had told us that we should save ourselves for marriage because if we didn't, it would be inviting multiple people into our marriage bed and that would be too much baggage and it's 'healthier' to wait."*
>
> *"Abstinence until after marriage."*
>
> *"It's a sin."*

Roughly half of the participants in that study reported messages that focused on protection. Unlike the abstinence-only approaches, protection-oriented messages did assume that the young woman would have sex, and instructed them on how to protect themselves when they did. However, most of these messages did not involve comprehensive or even always accurate information about sexual health. The most common protection message that people recalled was simply to "use a condom," but some reported more extensive messages like the need to "put your foot down" and "insist with guys" about condom usage. Many of these messages reinforced that safe sex was a woman's responsibility in (always assumed) heterosexual relationships.

Messages about both protection and abstinence position sex as physically and emotionally dangerous, but some offer instructions for how to manage that danger (either by taking steps toward safe sex, or by abstaining from sex). But many people report messages that just highlight the dangers of sex without offering any tips on how to manage or protect against that danger. Many of the memorable messages our participants reported in that study reflect outright myths or exaggerations about sexual health, almost echoing the *Mean Girls* satirical sex ed: "If you have sex, you will get pregnant and die." Many women describe often extreme messages related to avoiding pregnancy in their youth. A friend of Val's once shared that her mother said, "Don't come home to me if you get pregnant, or I'll kill you." Some participants in our study noted that it wasn't necessarily anything someone said to them, but the extreme graphics of STIs they saw in health classes that stuck with them.

Many of these messages shame or blame women for the social ills of sexual activity, or overstate the physical and emotional dangers without offering reasonable methods of how to mitigate or manage those risks, which can actively harm people. But many of them just failed to offer anything that would be particularly helpful in actually navigating sexual and relational life in adulthood. This duality is common for the types of messages that simply aren't helpful in our lives. Some of them directly hurt us (telling someone information that is untrue or feels hurtful), but some of them just aren't serving us anymore (Val's career messages).

In this particular study, we also assessed the impact of the memorable message on the individual's behavior and self-concept. We found five outcomes from the messages women received about sexual health: directly impacted behavior, negatively impacted self-concept, positively impacted self-concept, generally impacted self-concept, or no impact on self-concept or behavior.

About 40 percent of participants reported that the memorable message they received about sexual health *directly impacted* their sexual behavior or their communication behaviors. For instance, participants said that the messages they received did in fact lead them to abstain from sex in some cases, or made them choose one type of birth control over another. Some reported that it didn't necessarily impact their sexual behavior, but it did shape their communication choices; for instance, choosing not to come out to a family who expressed negative sentiment about LGBTQ+ sexuality.

Nearly the same percentage collectively noted that the memorable message impacted their self-concept in some way, whether negatively (18 percent), positively (10 percent), or generally (10 percent). For folks who said it impacted their self-concept, most did not explicitly identify a behavioral connection, saying that the message didn't necessarily influence their sexual or communication behaviors. But they might inform how an individual viewed and assessed those behaviors. For instance, those who felt it shaped their self-concept negatively would note that they sometimes felt bad about themselves when they had sex because they felt like sex was wrong.

About 10 percent of participants did imply that the messages they received, even though they remembered them, did not necessarily impact their self-concept or behavior. Although it was a smaller percentage of the overall sample, most of these folks highlighted that they believed they received messages from a wide variety of sources, which led to them forming their own opinions and beliefs rather than internalizing someone else's.

We use this study as a case in unpacking messages that hurt us because unlike many other subjects where we might find a variety of positive and negative messages, the messages that young people get about sex have historically been much more negative than positive. But messages can help or harm us about nearly any subject matter, so as you think through your own, feel free to consider any message that you feel is no longer serving you. It definitely doesn't have to be about sex or careers; these are just some of many examples of the kinds of messages that might not help us.

As another example, we turn to the pretty extensive memorable message research on body image and weight-related messages.

The Lasting Impact of Body and Weight Messages

Earlier we mentioned that a lot of memorable message research has studied the messages different groups of people receive about their bodies or their weight, and how it impacts body image, eating behavior, exercise behavior, and self-esteem, including Val's study, "Better to be depressed skinny than happy fat." There are dozens of memorable message studies about body image, dietary and exercise behavior, and related variables.

For instance, a recent study by Natasha Brown and LaShara Davis examined the memorable diet and exercise messages that Black women recalled. Many of the women in their study reported messages that encourage Black women to engage in broadly "healthy" behaviors in order to prevent disease or, often, to maintain a small body size.[8] Relatedly, researchers considering memorable messages about people in large bodies during the pregnancy process identified negative messages that women received about their bodies before pregnancy through postpartum. Those researchers identified harmful themes in their 237 participants' memorable messages about fat mothers being bad mothers, denial of competent treatment, weight-normative commentary about their bodies, and, positively, some more inclusive counter-narratives.[9]

Similarly, using memorable messages to understand that reference point for behavioral assessment we discussed earlier—how we compare our behaviors or traits to that ideal state memorable messages help form—a research study from 2017 looked at weight-associated memorable messages that college students receive.[10] An important finding from this study was that most participants felt their weight-related messages were positive or that the person sending the message was trying to help them. Considering that many of the messages participants reported indicated that they needed to be smaller, or no one would want them if they were overweight, these kinds of evaluations as generally well-meaning and positive highlight the complexity of interpreting messages that help or harm us. Empirically speaking, telling someone they need to be smaller for social reasons (no one will want to marry them; to be prettier or fit in better) is generally an ineffective procedure for producing healthy results,[11] and can backfire, resulting in mental health challenges or disordered eating behaviors.[12]

The body of research on what we remember people telling us about weight, exercise, health, and body size points to a fairly bleak picture, especially for women and for people from marginalized groups like Black women and LGBTQ individuals. They frequently receive messages that shame their bodies, tell them they must be small to be socially accepted, and that weight should primarily motivate their health behaviors. These messages can and do harm people who hear them. They can make individuals feel ashamed or insecure or unaccepted, and they can prompt mental health challenges or spur disordered eating behaviors. But most of us don't consider research science when deciding how we feel about something someone told us.

As Brown and Davis noted in their study:

> In addition, certain messages such as "thinner is better" and "Make sure you watch what you eat or you'll be fat like Grandma" contain fat phobic rhetoric. These messages are harmful to Black women as they focus on bodily appearance (which may not be an accurate representation of health) and align with historically negatively perceived views of this group of women [Strings, 2019].

These kinds of messages can do measurable harm to people who hear them.[13] They rarely motivate long-term, positive behavioral changes and often motivate long-term, negative mental and emotional health changes. Still, many of us who receive those messages, especially when we receive them from so many sources—media, doctors, friends, family—may have difficulty labeling them as harmful.

Identifying Harmful Messages

Short of a global pandemic to trigger emotional epiphanies, how can you identify the messages you received that have actively harmed you or that at least aren't helping? Especially in cases like Val's earlier story, or the many research studies on sex and body messages, we often incorporate these messages into our identity to such an extent that it's hard to separate ourselves from the message. We also don't always immediately have insight into when something isn't serving us. Starting to reconsider the messages that aren't helping us does require some serious self-reflection. Here, we'll guide you through one way to get started.

You may have, during the exercise in the last chapter, identified some messages that were not helpful to you during the major turning points in your life. When we asked what messages helped or encouraged you, you may have thought of some that didn't. Take a minute here to reflect on the exercise from Chapter 8, and record any messages that did not help you.

You can also consider any of the overtly harmful messages you've already identified in your life—perhaps those you brought up in past chapters, or that you thought of when reading about what memorable messages look like in different contexts.

By now, you might have identified some more obviously harmful memorable messages. While we hope it's not too long a list, it does vary person to person. Don't get too hung up on the length of your list. Give yourself permission to write as much or as little as fits your experience. Another way to identify your memorable messages is to ask yourself—what was your most memorable message in your life in general? What about your most memorable message about school? About work? About ethics? About relationships? Personality? Friends? Sex? Start writing down as many memorable messages as you can recall. From those messages, how did they impact your behavior, your self-concept, and your relationships?

Any of these messages that harmed or hurt you, or that simply failed to be useful in your life in a way that helped you (or are not serving you *currently* even if they did at one time), can fall under this category. Charting the way that messages impact your behavior, self-concept, and relationships helps tease out the more subtle unhelpful messages we might receive and hang onto. And again, this isn't universal by message. A message that for one person might be wildly helpful could be actively harmful to another person. We're different, and we have different emotional and communicative needs, and different contexts through which we experience life. Allow the process to help identify the messages that don't serve *you* anymore. If the consequence to your behavioral choices or how you assess your behavior, your self-concept, and/or your relationships is not what *you* want it to be, then permit yourself to categorize that message as harmful.

You may find, as you engage in this kind of self-reflection, that you find it harder to label messages as harmful than you did as helpful. We may often find it difficult to label our experiences this way, especially if we fall into the trap of comparing ourselves or our experiences to others. We might say "well, it's not as bad as…" and before you finish that thought, you're rejecting a part of your own experience. Try to hold back from judging yourself (or even from judging those who shared the messages with you) during this exercise, and instead embrace the freedom to label messages as they serve you—helpful or not.

We don't have to resent the sentiment of a message in order to acknowledge that this isn't something we want to continue carrying with us. Sometimes we can even appreciate it. For instance, Val experiences mostly gratitude to the people in her life who asked questions about her ambitions, expressed an interest in her goals, read her articles and chapters, and asked how work or school was going. They cared about her and cared about the thing she cared about. But those messages are not serving her today. We can acknowledge that while still feeling grateful or positive about the people who sent them to us. Similarly, many of the women in our research studies about sex and sexual health acknowledged that the teachers, parents, or older siblings who sent them relatively unhelpful messages about sex were probably just drawing from their own limited knowledge—not malice or ill intent.

This is important because one of the reasons we often hesitate to label messages as harmful (or even just as unhelpful) is because we worry about what it says about the message sender, or our relationship with them. If our moms, friends, or partners shared messages with us that hurt us or no longer help us, does that mean the relationships are bad or no longer help us? (It doesn't mean that.) Relationships are made of communication, but labeling a singular communication encounter in one way does not have to say anything about the entire relationship or the person who sent the message. While memorable messages obviously affect and reflect our relationships, as we have already discussed at length, this exercise is about *you* and how a message impacts you. Making the message and its impact about the person who sent it can take us down an unproductive rabbit hole at this stage.

That said, if you find that many of your memorable messages, especially those that are particularly hurtful, do come from one person or in the context of one relationship, that might say something not so great about that relationship. Even the most safe, warm, and loving relationships can hurt us sometimes—people have bad days and accidentally say something that hurts our feelings, but good relationships should not *routinely* hurt us.

As you generate your own list of messages that didn't help you, don't be afraid to think critically about messages that on their surface might seem positive and supportive. Allow yourself to think of the *outcome* of those messages, rather than the intent of the message sender. We understand that because memorable messages do often come closely attached to the person who sent them to us, we may feel that labeling a message as harmful or unhelpful means we are also labeling the person who said it as harmful or unhelpful. Remember, we can believe both that a message did not help us *and* that the person who said it had our best interests at heart at the same time. An unhelpful message does not need to mean a bad relationship; it can just mean an unhelpful message.

We can also acknowledge that the same message does not affect everyone the same way. Some people may be wildly grateful for someone showing support or interest in their career, or they really needed to receive a message that told them to focus on professional goals. If the messages helped them, then they were helpful. But for Val, the messages led to overly identifying with her career to a point where she lost other meaningful parts of herself. She can acknowledge nonjudgmentally that this was unhelpful for her, while holding space for others who might find the same messages extremely helpful. In this way, we are making the message about Val—not about the many people who shared those messages with her over the years. At one point, the meaning she took from those messages served her, and now it doesn't.

Further, you do not have to think of this exercise as all or nothing. A message can help you at one point in your life, then hurt you at another. The message might reflect elements of a warm, close relationship, but fail to light a fire at a time you need it. Nuance characterizes the messages that affect us. Give yourself the freedom to explore it, and the power to label those experiences as unhelpful if they aren't helpful or label them as harmful if they hurt you.

Of course, some messages are just overtly harmful. When someone does or says something that directly devalues us, criticizes unchangeable features of who we are (appearance, ability, or core identities), or approaches us with hostility or even violence in extreme cases, those kinds of messages clearly result in the experience of emotional hurt. Labeling them appropriately can help us begin the process of disrupting and rejecting them, which we'll talk about next.

Once you have this list, as you did in the last chapter, start to consider what your hurtful or unhelpful messages have in common. What connects them? Generate a bullet-point list of these characteristics. Once you have created a list of the common features of your hurtful, harmful, or otherwise just not-so-helpful messages, try to distill it into one declarative sentence: Messages that do not help me share the following features ... and then list them.

Disrupting Harmful Messages

Now, let's discuss what we can do with harmful messages now that we have identified some of our own. Labeling messages as harmful is half the challenge, but there is still another half. Charting how the message impacted you, then actively disrupting, releasing, or replacing the message allows us to take ownership of the communication we use and endorse. We'll talk more about that idea in the next chapter, but for now, here are some methods for addressing those not-so-helpful messages you have received throughout your life.

Focus on the Message Impact—Let Go of the Intention

First, as we noted earlier, our temptation when unpacking these messages often revolves around the person who sent them to us. We want to critique our parents, teachers, or friends (or, alternatively, we want to let them off the hook), identifying their motivations for sending us unhelpful messages as self-centered, controlling, or naive—or, alternatively, as well-meaning, loving, and supportive. These attributions answer the "why" questions about communication or behavior—why did they send us that message?[14] The answers to those why questions about a person's communication or behavior inform how we ultimately feel about it—the meaning we take from the message. However, the why question isn't actually that helpful in managing the *impact* of the message now, and ultimately, we're not going to know the answer to it. We're not mind readers or time travelers. We won't know exactly why anyone else does or says what they do or say. But most importantly, it doesn't really matter. We recommend practicing letting go of the perceived intention of the message sender. "Perceived" is an important word here—since we don't usually know the actual intention, it's just our perception of their intention. Although the relationship with the message sender is one of the reasons you likely remember that message in the first place, hanging onto *why* you think they sent it distracts and undermines the mission of ultimately moving past the messages that harm us.

Instead, focus on the message impact. In what ways did that message shape the decisions you made, or how you felt about those decisions? In what ways do these messages influence how you see

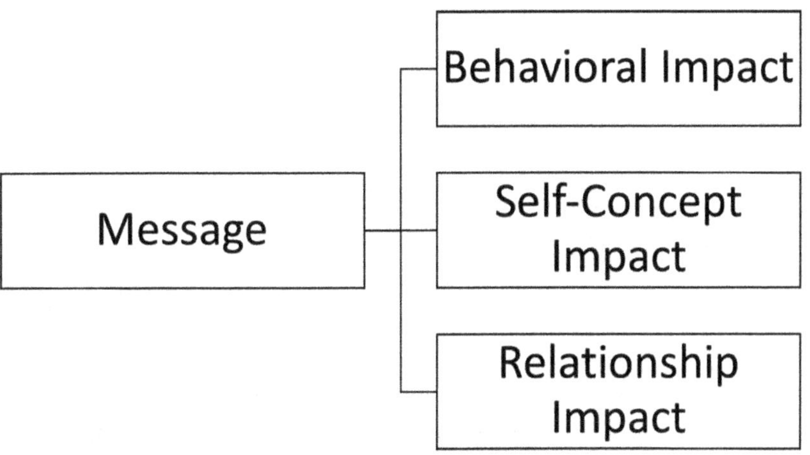

Memorable message impacts.

yourself? In what ways do these messages influence your feelings about relationships, or your relationships with specific people? To start, choose any one of the unhelpful or harmful messages you identified above.

From those impacts, consider how you know the behavior, self-concept, or relational outcomes were bad for you. For example, Val might consider "checking emails in the evening" to be a problematic behavioral and relational outcome *because* it distracts her from family time, which is what really makes her happy, or leads to feeling burned out and less present during both work and family time. Someone who is trying to let go of messages that tie their value as a person to their body size might identify behavioral problems like trying to account for every calorie they consume, or self-concept impacts like feeling bad about themselves because of what they look like. Take some space here to write out the "because" statements for what you have charted out so far.

This process of identifying and unpacking the messages you received and why they aren't helpful to you anymore is a part of the message disruption process we described earlier. Sometimes messages become disrupted by one significant event or experience. Sometimes they become disrupted because they are replaced with another message. For example, in some of our sex-message research, people note having heard something from a relational partner, a podcast, or a book that really spoke to them and made them reconsider their earlier memorable messages.[15] In many cases, this process can happen organically, as it did with Val's message and some of our participants. But for a lot of the messages we receive, nothing significant comes along to help us realize that it isn't good for us anymore. Repeating the process we described here on as many messages as you can will help you identify the messages you received that hurt you or just no longer help you, and identify how you know they aren't serving you anymore.

Letting go of messages that aren't serving us is certainly easier said than done. Once something is a part of our self-concept and memory, it takes some pretty intentional and consistent choices to move past it. That caveat is not meant to discourage us from trying. We wouldn't be writing this book if we didn't think it was possible, but are offering some realism as you do so yourself. This isn't an overnight exercise; it's a habit that takes time and intention to form and build. We also want to offer the caveat that for some really ingrained and really harmful messages, it can be beneficial to learn to manage or release them with the help of a therapist or support group. Particularly for messages rooted in traumatic experiences, doing this alone is not advised.

When we talk about releasing or replacing memorable messages that no longer serve us, we aren't talking about taking a magic eraser to your memory and scrubbing out a piece of it. We are talking about releasing ourselves from the harmful *impact* of those messages. We can't control what someone says to us, and you can't change the past, but you can learn from it and make choices that do serve you and your goals in the future.

Building off your last exercise, make a list of goals for how you want to address or change a message that harmed you. For instance, Val might write under behavior, "Don't check emails outside of working hours"; "Avoid overly talking about work with family and friends"; and "Prioritize being present when I'm with my spouse, family, or friends." Under self-concept, she might write, "Do not use professional traits or accomplishments to describe myself," and so on. These can include things you're already doing, if this is a message you're already working on, or it can include things you might want to change or consider in the future.

Another strategy for managing our more harmful messages involves offering a replacement message. As we stated earlier, sometimes a new message disrupts an old message. Whenever we think or call upon a message we have identified as not helping us or hurting us, try to actively recall a more productive message instead. For instance, in our research on sex messages, participants recalled replacing messages that told them they were responsible for abstaining from sex with messages that told them they could always say no if they wanted to.[16] That might seem like a subtle shift, but the emphasis on empowerment and consent—that they shouldn't have sex unless they want to have sex, rather than they shouldn't have sex, period—enabled them to disrupt their less useful memorable message and replace it with one that actually serves them. Consider some more helpful messages you have received that might replace some of your more harmful ones.

In what ways can those helpful messages impact your behavior, self-concept, or relationships? Do you have goals for how you might want them to?

In the next two chapters, we'll continue this process. Drawing from both our helpful and harmful messages, we will learn how to actively shape our behavior and identity scripts and take ownership of both the messages we have received and those that we send to others.

10

Agency and Taking Ownership of the Messages We Hold Onto

In the last two chapters, we began to think critically about the memorable messages we have received and how they helped and hurt us. The purpose of reflecting on the messages that hurt us is to find ways to let go of the impact those messages had so they no longer hold the same power over us. We reflect on messages that help us so we can embrace and call upon the memorable moments that bring us peace, wisdom, or strength. We will continue in this chapter to explore what it means to take agency and ownership over the messages we hold onto and, in the next chapter, those we ultimately share with others.

Sometimes taking agency of our memorable messages means first acknowledging we need to let go of a message that no longer serves us, as we discussed in the last chapter, and replace it with one that does. To begin, Val will share a brief story about a memorable message she realized she needed to replace about the role of grief in her life.

Ghosts and Grief on Halloween

Anyone who knows me, or spends five seconds in my skull- and bat-decorated office, knows Halloween is my absolute favorite holiday. I love the way Halloween affords the freedom to embrace weirdness, creativity, and silliness even for those who may not describe themselves as all that artistically inclined. I love the crisp air, the last few leaves on the trees, the combination of glitter and harmlessly spooky aesthetics. Of course, candy, pumpkin-spice-flavored anything, and apples don't hurt either.

But the real reason Halloween holds such a special place in my heart is because of my grandmother. I grew up five houses down the street from my grandparents on my mother's side. They helped raise me and I was really close to both of them throughout my childhood and into my early adulthood. My grandmother, Gram, as my many cousins and I called her, loved Halloween.

I recall the first time she let me help update her yearly display of recycled milk-jug skeletons with my slightly older, artistically inclined cousin, validating a growing knack for arts and crafts. Much of my family gathered at her house every Halloween. I always rushed back at least a half an hour early from my own trick-or-treating as a kid to be sure I could pass out some of her candies (they were always better than whatever my parents were giving out). I had pictures of my Halloween costumes from every year of my childhood at the same backdrop in her living room, in front of a decorated mantel lined with Halloween decor and my and my cousins' yearly school pictures. I remember giggling with my cousins and friends while "Monster Mash" played in the background and Gram insisted on checking our Halloween candies for razor blades (that was something parents were worried about in the '90s). Halloween was a party in my family, a time for closeness, encouragement, and laughter.

Years before my Gram passed away, the Halloween tradition dwindled, a common experience for family traditions shepherded by a family matriarch. When Gram was unable to continue the Halloween traditions, they faded. The kids in our family grew up, and she became ill in my late teen years. It was a long time before I watched my mom pop back into celebration-mode come October 31. In part, that's because we receive a lot of memorable messages that tell us that thinking about things that make us sad is bad. My grandmother passed away almost a decade ago, actually around the same time I met my spouse. When she first died, I didn't really want to talk about it. Thinking about her made me sad, and I found the sadness in many ways distracting.

A few years after she died, I decided that I wanted to cook my Gram's "famous" mashed potatoes for Thanksgiving, so I texted my aunt for the recipe. While preparing Thanksgiving dinner that year, I mentioned to my spouse that Gram taught me how to cook. Growing up, my family gathered at my grandmother's every Sunday for dinner. While I helped chop vegetables for her salad, she would always tell me, "Garlic is how we keep our family healthy. Make sure to put a lot in there." I still hear her voice instructing care when I'm mincing garlic or flipping pancakes (although she would probably be turning over in her grave if she saw my often dairy- and gluten-free cooking these days).

When I disclosed that detail to my spouse, apparently for the first time, I remember Sam saying, "You never really talk about her, I assumed you weren't that close," and expressed some surprise when I explained that we were actually quite close when I was growing up. She watched my brother and me many days after school. I spent tons of nights at her house either out of necessity or because I wanted to be there. I asked her for advice and support too many times to count (and she offered me unsolicited advice and support many more times than that, as people who love us tend to do). She encouraged my love for cooking (always putting me to work in her kitchen) and art and writing (her basement was practically a gallery to my childhood doodles and poems).

When I explained to my spouse that this was actually a pretty close relationship, not a distant relative, they expressed probably reasonable surprise given how little I talked about her up until that point. I responded that I "may have a tendency to compartmentalize." To which Sam said, "Well, when you're ready to unpack that compartment, I'm here." As soon as I heard the words, a new memorable message began to shake and replace those that told me to think of my grief as an inconvenience.

Like nearly everyone else who lost someone close to them, many people feel that there's a pretty tight timeline on tolerance for grief. Being sad is okay for a little while, but then life goes on and you should too. My spouse's message helped counter some of that for me, and reminded me that at any point that I wanted to, I was allowed to feel how I felt about it. Having space in a relationship to feel the full range of feelings brought by thinking about people we love who are no longer with us also allowed me to understand that sadness isn't the only part of grief.

Now, around Halloween, I bring my Gram up as much as possible. While sitting outside and passing out candy to the children in my own neighborhood, I talk about my childhood traditions, how much Gram loved the holiday, and share pictures of our family kiddos in costumes. I talk about it with my mom and with anyone else who will listen and let myself feel how I feel about it. Now, with enough time and distance, it's more nostalgia than sadness. Halloween is still my favorite, and I let my grief, memories, and presence play together. I invoke the memorable moments now as a way to continue feeling close to someone who meant a lot to me and to keep my Gram's memory alive during her favorite time of year.

Reframing grief, a subject entering popular discussion lately thanks to celebrity accounts,[1] offers a common example of the ways we can actively choose to adjust the messages we accept, and those we reject, and change our behavioral scripts to better serve us. To illustrate, let's talk through some of the recent research that explored the important subject of messages we receive while grieving.

Grief is tough, and losing people we love is one of those turning point moments when the messages we receive from others during those hard times can actively help or hurt us. A research study by our friend Heather Carmack and her colleague Josie DeGroot[2] looked at the specific traits of messages that helped or hurt people in mourning. Perhaps unsurprisingly, their research found that helpful messages contained certain traits that differed from harmful messages. Helpful messages in the context of grieving included those that afforded those in mourning space to grieve and feel their feelings. Hurtful messages attempted to explain or rationalize the death, or in some other way minimized or made the loss seem smaller.

For communication scientists, this isn't necessarily a surprising finding. In general, during tough times, we respond better to messages that help us process and allow us to feel our feelings in all their messy complexity than those that try to minimize, reject, or explain our feelings. Person-centered messages that that validate our emotional response and encourage us to think through and elaborate on those feelings[3] ("That sounds really scary and challenging, it makes sense that you feel that way. Let's talk about it" or Val's spouse's "When you're ready to unpack that compartment") can lead us to think differently about our situation.[4] We tend to prefer these kinds of messages to those that minimize or criticize our feelings ("Get over it" or "Well they were old weren't they?" in response to grief), or those that try to distract us from our feelings ("Let's take your mind off of it").

In addition to embracing those messages that organically help us and finding ways to reject or replace those that harm us, sometimes we need to get creative in seeking out messages that best meet our needs. This is especially true if we realize we are in need of a memorable message. We don't have to wait to just experience them. To illustrate, Angela will share memorable messages she intentionally sought during the pandemic.

Intentionally Seeking Memorable Messages

In the midst of the Covid-19 pandemic, like Val and nearly everyone else in the country, I found myself in an existential crisis struggling with my identity and my contribution to family, to my students, and to society at large. In an effort to cope with the stress of an ongoing crisis, one of the things I decided to do was to ask a few of my mentors and friends, most of whom were 10 or more years older than me, what they had learned about themselves and their lives. I figured they'd lived through more than I had, so they could offer some sage advice on finding stillness and grounding, something I needed in the moment of stress.

Two of the people I queried included my older sister, whom I am very close to, and my college professor, mentor, and now friend, Dr. B-H. Dr. B-H has been in my life since the junior year of my undergraduate degree. Both women's words became the impetus for wanting to do more research on menopause experiences among women—a research project Val and I have been engaged in the last few years. Through my conversations and guidance with my sister and Dr. B-H, I found an abundance of wisdom in caring less what others think of you that manifests when you are older. What was truly special is that Dr. B-H, or Deb, as I call her, sent me a list that included her eight life lessons. I've copied and tucked them in my journal as daily affirmations.

1. *Give yourself more time to do a task—rushing can lead to negative consequences.*
2. *Only take responsibility for yourself (unless it is a child we're talking about).*

3. *Faith is not church. Don't trust the people who say otherwise to give you spiritual advice.*

4. *Finances—time to work for money is running out. Pare down, focus on the truly important, and save money.*

5. *Begin to assess and celebrate your accomplishments, bearing in mind that all we do is temporary anyway. Only the work we do in people's lives has the potential to outlive us.*

6. *Admiration and loyalty. Decide which you would rather have.*

7. *We're forced to rely less on the physical, which makes the intellectual and spiritual more important.*

8. *Think about how you want to live in your 70s and 80s—how can they be meaningful?*

Of all of these, number 5 is one of my favorites—it reminds me of something my mother would say.

Memorable messages often happen by accident, but they can also occur on purpose by seeking out messages from people we respect and admire. When we want to draw upon messages that fill us with hope, drive, and comfort, sometimes we have to take the wheel. There can be value in just asking the people we respect what they think, or seeking out wisdom from authors or speakers who fill us with inspiration. Besides, most of us love giving advice—and being asked for advice makes us feel good and valued. In addition to having the benefit of access to new, positive, and helpful memorable messages, asking for them can grow our close relationships with the person who sends them to us.

Keeping in mind what helps and what doesn't when it comes to our communication, let's talk about actively shifting the scripts associated with those messages you find not so helpful. Continuing on the work you did in the last two chapters, here we advocate claiming agency in the process of hearing and shaping our own memorable messages. We encourage you to think of communication not as something that just happens *to* you, but as a process within which you are an active participant.

Rewriting Our Own Scripts

Memorable messages impact our identity and behavior in many ways through the formation of cognitive scripts—those templates for how we see ourselves that guide our actions and help us assess them. For instance, we have identity scripts for what it means to be someone's spouse, parent, friend, or child. From those identity scripts, we develop behavioral scripts for guiding us through interactions associated with those roles ("Mothers take care of their children"). Both identity and behavior scripts can stem from memorable messages we receive starting in childhood and throughout our lifespan, and they are not always associated with specific social roles; sometimes they just affect how we see ourselves overall. For example, messages of perseverance and resilience might lead to identity scripts whereby you see yourself as an independent and resilient person,[5] or to behavioral scripts that discourage asking for help or more positively promote problem-solving.

For another example, consider a common behavioral script that many of us develop to distract people from their feelings. As we mentioned earlier, communication scientists advocate an effective way to verbally respond to people's emotional needs with person-centered messages.[6] Person-centered messages are what they sound like—the degree to which a message centers the person meant to receive the message and their experience. In much of the research on the effectiveness of person-centered messages (which finds pretty consistently they are associated with a host of positive personal and relational outcomes and are an effective form of emotional support[7]), person-centeredness focuses on an individual's subjective experience of their own stressors.[8] This is an academic way of saying that person-centered messages center on what a specific person feels like they are going through—what their emotional response is, how they feel about something. That might sound obvious, but for many of us, our instinct when someone shares something emotionally heavy with us is to home in on situational details—who said or did what, do you agree or disagree with them—or to distract from the emotions altogether.

Those person-centered messages that offer space for unpacking our emotional responses are a highly effective way to respond to emotional situations, but they're not necessarily the most common. That's because for most of us, we develop behavioral scripts that steer us away from more vulnerable forms of communication, having internalized cultural memorable messages that tell us any form of discomfort might be bad (and feeling big feelings with someone can sure as heck be uncomfortable).

As a result, our behavioral scripts when someone shares heavy news with us might encourage responses that attempt to distract the person from their feelings. For example, we might suggest a literal distraction like "Let's take your mind off of it and go for a drink"; "Let's see a movie"; or "Why don't you come out with us and stop thinking about it for a bit?" Often, these behavioral scripts are well-meaning, intended to bring some comfort. And sometimes we want to be distracted from our own feelings—especially in the case of something ongoing. But ultimately, they avoid people's emotions and lack empathy.

Similarly, many of us develop what Brené Brown[9] and many empathetic communication researchers[10] have described as the tendency to silver-line. This behavioral script looks at something like hearing rough news from someone, and attempting to suggest it isn't so bad. For instance, when receiving news of the death of a loved one, especially a grandparent, someone might respond, "At least they lived a long life." Brown gives the advice that empathetic responses rarely start with "At least."[11]

If reading that made you cringe, perhaps recalling instances where you may have responded to a friend's grief, a breakup, or rough patches in a career or relationship with an "at least" statement, you are in the company of most other people. Feeling *with* someone involves accessing our own vulnerable emotions, and that takes courage.[12] It also departs from how most of us learn to interact with and comfort others. Consider how we often teach children to interact with other people's big feelings. When someone in their life is sad, we often instruct them to go "cheer them up." We incorporate these messages into our identity scripts as friends, partners, or family—helping our loved ones rally during hard times. In doing so, we develop behavioral scripts like this one—to distract someone from difficult feelings or help them "cheer up."

But just because we have an instinct to avoid those big feelings doesn't mean we have to listen to that instinct. We can change our behavioral scripts to avoid these tendencies, but doing so takes an *active* decision and a commitment to practicing it. We can revise our scripts to lean into rather than away from big feelings, and revise our memorable messages so that they encourage identity and behavioral scripts that make us more effective communicators.

Improving our empathetic responses may offer a good starting point, but we can scrape off the sticky messages that no longer serve us and revise our associated scripts about any subject. Earlier in this book, we asked you to document some of your own scripts. In the last two chapters, we thought critically about how memorable messages help us and hurt us, with the goal of embracing messages that help us and letting go, rejecting, or replacing messages that hurt us. To that end, let's reconsider those identity and behavior scripts further.

Remember, scripts are more or less our brain on autopilot.[13] We don't have to follow them, and we can actively choose which scripts we want to endorse and those we want to reject by becoming aware of them. That awareness affords us some measure of control,[14] allowing us to change course. Or, given the metaphor of scripts—to literally rewrite them. While you can't magically erase the memorable messages that helped form those initial scripts, you can absolutely change how they continue to influence you and make choices that reinforce the messages that serve you and reject the ones that don't.

Psychologists call this subject metacognition[15]—thinking about thinking. That's what we're asking you to do here. Turn off the autopilot, and think critically about *what* you think, *how* you think, and *why* you think that way. Specifically, think about the memorable messages that led to thinking the way you do. Doing so can help bring to focus why we fall into patterns of thought or behavior that help us or hurt us or help clarify what we need instead.

Let's take some of the messages you identified in the last chapter. Look specifically at how you believe those messages affected your behavior or your self-concept.

The chart above is an example of how you might begin to map out the behavioral and identity scripts associated with particular messages. You can choose any message you receive and do this for yourself. In this example, we chose the message "Friends help each other feel better"—a prescriptive message (that tells us what to do) about what being a friend means, with both behavioral and identity implications.

This message is probably well-meaning—who wouldn't want to feel better, after all? But messages like this can result in communication

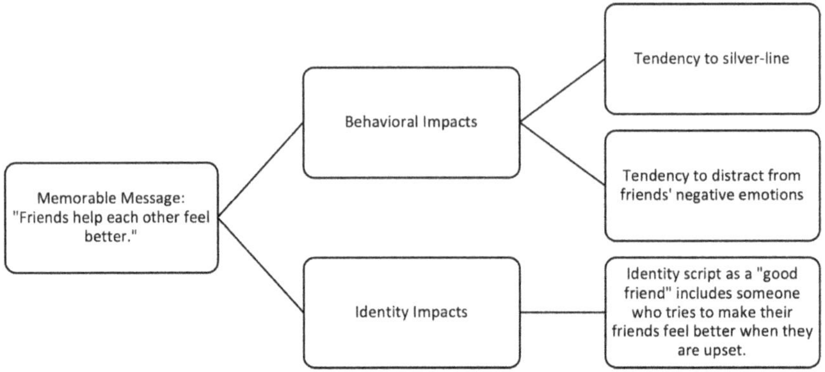

Behavioral script model.

practices that don't actually help anyone, and undermine our capacity to be empathetic with one another. So, if we find ourselves engaging in behaviors that aren't serving us as well as they could, we can actively reframe and adjust these scripts. For example, we can revise the identity script by deciding that friends just help each other, period.

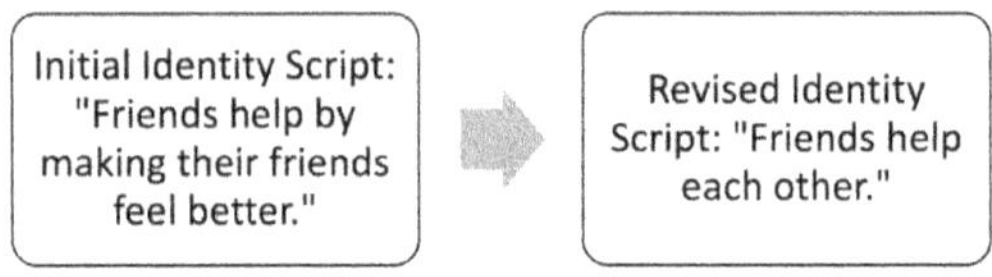

Revised behavioral script model.

Actively reframing how we think about things, or rewriting the scripts we learn from our memorable messages, is a choice. Consider some of the scripts associated with the behavior and identity outcomes that you identified in the last chapter. Take some time to map out a few of them.

Now, consider in what ways those scripts could be revised to better suit your needs and goals. Take time to undertake that revision, or to literally rewrite your scripts.

For another example, Angela will share one of her own memorable messages about age and aging and how she revised an identity script:

The frequently uttered memorable message "age ain't nothing but a number" served two functions in the Black community I grew up in. First, it was a way to note that we often looked younger than our actual numerical age. Second, it was a way to remind you that you should live as if you were young ... not tired, or aging, but like you still had the playfulness, agility, and mental acuity of a youngster.

Throughout this book, I frequently shared stories about my mother because the messages she shared really encapsulate so much of who I've grown to be as an adult—as I look back it feels like my mother was before her time in her ideas and knowledge. It was my mother who took me to play tennis, and when she'd taught me all she could, she enlisted my cousin Kevin, who played on the professional tennis circuit in Toledo, to continue to instruct me. It was my mother who decided to start running in her 60s—she'd heard it could be a useful addition to her other exercises and help manage her diabetes. She encouraged me to join her. I did and would go on to keep running as a primary exercise outlet into my 50s. It was my mother who took me and my cousins swimming in the summer and made sure we learned the proper techniques even though she could not fully teach them. My mother understood my curiosity and expected that I'd take this knowledge to the next level. I did! I remember attending a Bible camp where I took lifeguarding lessons as my extracurricular activity—I was simply curious about this water experience; didn't know it was something I could do but was damn determined to learn. So I signed up. After a week of camp, I was a certified junior lifeguard. Even with occasional lapses over the years, I kept this certification until I was in my 60s. I was always proud when I got my red and white card from the Red Cross that pronounced me as a certified lifeguard and water safety instructor. In my 20s, I would go on to get certified as a swim instructor and over the course of time teach everyone from adult learners, children, to "mom and me" swimming lessons. Even my husband's three children would have to learn to swim—it was my expectation as their stepmother. My curiosity led me to get my certifications as a water aerobics instructor where I taught exercise classes in the water. I remain a physically active person and value continuing to learn new activities. In a way, doing this over my lifespan feels partly the result of "age ain't nothing but a number" as well as the message to stay playful, curious, and agile.

Like most people, Angela received plenty of memorable messages that valorized youth and demonized aging. Having been immersed in the advice and role model of her mother as well as older women in her life, she intentionally came to realize the beauty and grace of growing older and the wisdom found in life experience that affirmed her curiosity, playfulness, and creativity. She chose not to associate those traits with youth, but rather to embody them throughout her lifespan through sport and play. As a result, she was able to replace early identity scripts that minimized the value of aging and emphasized the importance of youth with scripts that embraced age and aging. She also came to value physical activity like running, swimming, and tennis because of messages associated with the value of youth.

While the early message may have intended to suggest that being an active person meant being young, Angela has maintained an involvement in these activities throughout her life. As a result, she takes that memorable message to now embody values of playfulness, curiosity, and agility that she can explore through sport and bodily movement. The emphasis on those values, rather than age, is an example of revising an identity script.

The ability to revise an identity script, especially one reinforced by cultural messages like that, requires both serious self-reflection and intention. We have to engage in some forgiveness for believing a message that didn't serve us (or that served us at one point, but no longer does), and think deeply about why we bought that message in the first place. Finding counterexamples, or intentionally seeking out messages from others to help establish identity scripts that better meet your current needs, can also be helpful. In the case of Angela's message, she revised the identity scripts that active=youth with a script that valued activity along with age.

As we mentioned earlier, our research team has been interviewing women about their menopause experiences for the last few years. Like Amelia's story we shared earlier, many of our participants recounted memorable messages that made them feel unsure of themselves, bad about their symptoms, like they shouldn't talk about menopause, or like their difficulties burdened others. We find this problem reflected in many gendered health experiences that we research—kids going through puberty[16] and learning to manage their menstrual cycles[17]—women receive a lot of messages that instruct them to minimize their discomfort, ignore difficult symptoms, or avoid talking about their bodily experiences. It can make talking about women's health feel taboo.[18] Those messages not only don't serve them, they actively hurt people who may need medical assistance or, minimally, have a right to talk about their bodies and their lives.

Sometimes organically or out of necessity, and sometimes with intention, we can revise the scripts that stem from those messages. Once we acknowledge what the messages are and how they have affected us, we can choose to change the resulting behavioral and identity scripts. First, we need to acknowledge what identity and behavioral scripts those messages created. For instance, the abundance of memorable messages women receive about their health experience may result in problematic behavioral scripts that instruct them not to trust their symptoms, not to ask for help, or not to talk about their experiences.[19,20,21] Once we identify why those scripts don't help us, we can actively rewrite them. For example, we may consider instead: "I trust my body to tell me when something is wrong." "I deserve to be listened to about my health." Accepting our rewritten scripts probably won't happen overnight. Sometimes, like with the memorable messages we initially received, they need to be repeated. But we can do this intentionally too. We can say it to ourselves, we can ask others in our lives to repeat it back to us, we can journal and write it down, or we can look ourselves in the mirror and say it aloud.

It's a little bit of a cliche that while we can't control what people say or do, we can control how we react, but that is the message we hope you take away from this chapter. It's easy to feel like communication is something that just happens to us—we received the messages we received, and they influenced us as they did, and that's that. But we don't have to accept every message we hear, or remain influenced even by those we previously internalized. You are an active part of the communication process, and an active participant in the memorable messages you hold onto and call upon.

11

Moving Forward— The Memorable Messages We Send

As we conclude this book and reflect on the messages we send to and receive from others, we want to describe a memorable message shared between the two of us. We have known each other and worked together for about 13 years at the time of this writing. During this time, Angela frequently shares the motto "be still." Given the novelty of a shared memorable message between the two of us, we thought it a good example to transition from memorable messages as a receiver to memorable messages as a sender. Here, we reflect on the memorable message from the varying perspectives of sender and receiver within the communication process.

Angela's Perspective on "Be Still"

Cautious as I was about others' intentions, I was still a curious and investigatory kid. I wanted to touch everything, see what it felt like, and know the "why" for everything. When I was a little kid, my curiosity and unwavering fearlessness would often result in small and sometimes big catastrophes. I heard on a continuous loop, "Angela, sit down," "Angela, get out of that," "Angela, don't touch that." My siblings, who were often responsible for keeping an eye on me, would hear from my mother, "Where is Angela?" or "Who was watching Angela, where did she go?"

I have heard the story of how my older siblings all got into trouble one day because they were supposed to be watching me and were not properly paying attention to where I was or what I'd gotten into. Well, I somehow got out of the house and walked down the sidewalk to my mother's bus stop. It was not a difficult route and I'd likely remembered it from prior walks to meet her when she arrived home from work. At any rate, it wasn't something I was allowed to do as I was only five years old at the time. My mother would tell this story to me when I was older, especially when all my siblings were present. "Remember that time you guys were not watching Angela and she got out of the house and walked to my bus stop?" She shares, "I hear the folks on the bus asking who is that little child walking down the sidewalk by themself?" My mother, weary and exhausted from a late-night shift, looking out the bus window and realizing "that's Angela ... that's my baby." My siblings all got into trouble that day.

Over and over my mother would tell me to "be still," which meant slow down, don't hurt yourself, don't hurt someone else, don't be impulsive, don't rush the process, be aware of your surroundings, take a breath or two before you act.... All this to calm my often-misplaced energy and ground me. It is from here that I adopted these words.

Finding comfort in those words my mother shared to calm a curious and impulsive child, I even have it tattooed on my arm—"be still"—as a reminder that when I get wired up or feel even a bit overwhelmed that first I need to still myself. I share those two words often with my mentees, friends, and family, noting that first and foremost stillness can be a place of peace.

Val's Perspective on "Be Still"

I don't remember the first time I heard Angela say the words "be still"—it must have been at least a decade ago—but I do remember the most recent. Our lab has a group chat with all of the faculty and research associates. A common echo in that chain is #bestill, repeating our shared memorable message from our mentor and friend. The refrain almost characterizes the mentorship Angela provided to me and the rest of our group. Certainly, the way I interpret and internalize this message differs from others, but for me, it has always been a needed reminder to slow down, be intentional about my personal and professional choices, and be present in the moment.

Angela and I first met in 2012 at Emerson College, where at the time I was one of her graduate students. Our relationship evolution from mentor-mentee to writing partners and colleagues shifted gradually over more than a decade of research collaboration. Like many who value the messages received from their teachers or mentors, her memorable message "be still" guided her approach to teaching me to navigate academic writing and publishing, my professional trajectory, and the challenges and triumphs of a career in higher education.

Like many careers, it is very easy to get a little "go go go" when it comes to academia, to move swiftly between projects and goals. Although I'm sure this wasn't the first time she said it to me ("be still" most definitely meets the conditions of repetition; Angela says it to me, her students, and our lab all the time), but my first salient memory of hearing "be still" occurred while planning one of our first research projects. As a new researcher and graduate student, my ambition would have stuffed a million questions and ideas into that project if given the room. Angela never actively discouraged students, and never told me to calm down, but she did tell me to "be still," and consider the power and value of even just one question—if it's a good question.

I remember hearing it again when we went through the process of publishing our first journal article together. The peer-review process can be overwhelming and discouraging, and I remember her teaching me how to navigate and incorporate feedback, and how to find wisdom in critique. (Another memorable message she delivered during that time period, "Someone who takes the time to write pages of feedback is really taking your work seriously," helped reframe criticism and is a cornerstone of my writing and editing process to this day, one I routinely share with my own students.)

Around the same time that we published that article, it won a top paper award from a local conference. As a doctoral student at that point, my instinct was to quickly add the award to my CV and then return to getting the paper published. Angela repeated "be still" and reminded me of the value of celebrating and experiencing those moments.

Our lab consists of a diverse group of women from wildly different personal and professional backgrounds at differing levels of education and occupation. At one point or another, I am pretty sure all of them have repeated her "be still" to our group, to me, to each other. It's a memorable message that many of us share and that in some ways shapes the identity of our professional and personal space.

Throughout this book, we have focused on the memorable messages we receive from others, why we remembered them, and how they impacted us. Then, we moved on to how we can make more active choices when it comes to the memorable messages we choose to endorse. We can actively rewrite the behavioral and identity scripts that memorable messages leave, and use that to guide more fulfilling personal, relational, and professional choices.

As we conclude this book, we want to take this chapter to remember that while we receive many memorable messages, the communications we deliver to others can also become *their* memorable messages. All of us are both source and recipient of memorable messages many times throughout our life. We opened this chapter by describing a memorable message that the two of us share from different perspectives—as sender (Angela) and receiver (Val). Improving our relationship to memorable messages involves examining not only the messages we receive, but also those we share. In an effort to move forward on this journey, we take some time here to outline considerations we ought to make in our daily communication to encourage becoming someone else's helpful memorable message, and avoid delivering the kinds of messages that people need to reject or reclaim.

Importantly, our varied perspectives on the phrase highlight the fickle nature of communication. Angela learned and repeated "be still" to ground the impulses of childlike curiosity and enthusiasm. Val has adopted it to ground ambition and celebrate the little moments. Both of us find grounding in the idea, but in differing ways that reflect our own needs, paths, and personalities. A lesson from the differences in our perspectives reflects the way communication works and an axiom we shared earlier in the book: meanings are in people. But often, we form that meaning as both sender and receiver without much attention or intention.

As communication scientists, we know that many of the problems people have that stem from challenges in communication—misunderstandings, poor listening, lack of empathy in messages—often come down to when we allow our communication to run on autopilot.[1] We have lamented this challenge from the perspective of the message recipient for the last 10 chapters. At this point, we hope you feel this text has helped you to develop some tools to reclaim your agency and take ownership of the messages you receive and internalize. The work of choosing which messages to embrace and which to reject and how we will let them affect us is ongoing. We hope you feel ready to tackle the communications you receive in life and make better use of them. However, we also all too often let that autopilot take charge when we *deliver* messages. For the rest of this chapter, we'll talk about how to make the most of the memorable messages we might (knowingly or unknowingly) send to others.

Complementary and Peer Relationships

For individuals in positions of higher status or authority—parents, grandparents, aunts, uncles, organizational or community leaders, teachers, mentors, even older siblings—we might think intentionally about the kinds of memorable messages we hope to leave with the people in our complementary roles (children, students, younger siblings). But the messages we hope will be memorable and those that actually are may not always be the same messages. Here, we want to talk a bit about the messages we deliver that ultimately help socialize others.

In this book, we have discussed the idea of anticipatory socialization—memorable messages help prepare us for circumstances we'll face in the future. They shed light on what we can expect to occur, how we ought to behave, help develop resiliencies or coping strategies, or serve as words of warning and caution. By now, you have had time to reflect on the socializing messages you received yourself—how they prepared you, or failed to prepare you, for the life you have ended up living. But we also deliver socializing messages to others. For parents or grandparents and people in roles like teacher or community leader, this probably isn't news. You already hope that what you say to your children, grandchildren, students, or members of your organization helps shape them into someone prepared to engage in the world, and a lot of it does. A significant body of memorable message research[2] has explored the impact of parental memorable messages, as parents fill an important role as one of our primary socializing systems. They teach us a lot about how to navigate the world. Let's elaborate on a few of these studies.

About 20 years ago, a team of researchers investigated the memorable messages young adults received from their parents about work, family, and balance—they also wanted to find out if the messages received by men and women differed (they do).[3] By studying more than 900 memorable messages, this research found that parents often advise their young adults to pursue career pathways that they would find fulfilling and to balance the role of work and family in their lives. However, young women received more messages about balance than young men, often instructing them to prioritize family or even just anticipated family responsibilities down the line. Similar findings, parental messages emphasizing pursuing ambitions, have been repeated in several other studies since.[4,5]

Work, family, and school are frequent topics of the memorable messages that parents deliver to their children and young adults. But parents also socialize their children to understand morality—what's right and wrong—through memorable messages, sometimes unintentionally.[6] In a different research study, messages about morality became most memorable when delivered interpersonally, when it was just the parent and child without any other audience present, and when delivered both face to face and at home. This study also found that the messages were most often spontaneous—parents did not plan to deliver the moral message. Communication perceived as more spontaneous often feels more sincere,[7] so young people may be more likely to buy the message if they don't feel like their parents were lecturing them.

If you find yourself in a position where you *want* to send someone memorable messages—and certainly, that position exists for many of us—lessons from these research studies can help. Messages are more memorable when delivered in the context of interpersonal conversation—when two people are talking one-on-one rather than in group contexts. That means for important conversations, setting time aside to talk can be meaningful.

It can also be helpful to remember to be mindful about the ways that our perceptions of identities like gender can influence the messages we send to others. Although, optimistically, gender differences in memorable parental messages about work seem to be less pronounced than in earlier research studies,[8] memorable socializing messages may differ by gender in other contexts. Most memorable message research from the last decade does not compare groups, but rather focuses on only one (the study only surveys women, or only surveys men). Thus, while we can talk about differences those studies find, we don't know how meaningful the differences actually are from a research perspective. But we do know that gender remains a powerful socializing source, and families remain an important socializer.

Mindful communication involves avoiding common stereotypes that reduce people to singular traits. For example, assuming that knowing a detail like a person's gender means that we know what they will be interested in, what skills they will exhibit, or what values they will hold. Communication is always most effective when it's tailored to the individual, something we'll elaborate on shortly. So, in all, it's good advice to check ourselves to ensure we are not unintentionally repeating stereotypical messages that may ultimately become memorable to someone.

This doesn't mean we have to avoid talking about identity. For some people, their gender, race, religion, or age are important parts of who they are, and talking about them can be really meaningful. For instance, throughout this book, Angela shared several examples about messages that came from being raised in a Black community in her early years that were important to her. But these messages were balanced by many that reflected her idiosyncrasies. We are suggesting that it's worth asking ourselves if a message we might send is stemming from assumptions we hold about a person rooted in ideas that reduce them to a single trait (such as "woman") or if we are crafting comprehensive messages that capture the whole of who a person is and who they could be, which can include those elements of identity—but also so much more. Angela received messages about being Black, being a woman, aging, all of which matter to her immensely—but she also received messages about being curious, grounded, and sometimes cautious that are both interwoven with those identities and exist independent of them.

People find comprehensive messages that cover more ground—that allow for nuance and more information—more effective than single-point or reductionist messages.[9] But messages that encourage us to embrace the whole of who we are and who we can be most certainly will not come from stereotypes. Stereotypical ideas permeate our culture—we hear them daily from so many sources that it would be hard to avoid. This is why it's important, especially when talking to people for whom we may be a source of a memorable message, to be sure that our own messages reflect a comprehensive design rather than reiterating stereotypes they will certainly hear elsewhere.

Consider again the ways in which messages become memorable: Utility, repetition, and relationships. We value messages from people we care about, respect, and look up to. The relational component plays a significant role in these messages, but so does the message's actual usefulness to the recipient and the frequency of its repetition, both by you as the source and by others in their life.

Sometimes a singular message, said by the right person at the right moment, even just once, passes the test of time and stays with us. Be mindful of what you communicate to the people who look up to you. The words you say can always become someone else's memorable message. We recommend considering the characteristics you identified in Chapter 8. What are the common features of *your* helpful memorable messages? Be intentional in your communication, and keep those traits front and center when crafting messages to others.

Think critically about the values embedded in the messages you share and repeat. What *is* the message? We hope that by this point in this book, you understand that messages are more than just the words that someone says. Language, nonverbal elements, and context work together to form a core message—what does someone really mean by what they say? Consider not only the words, tone, and context, but the values and meaning that underlie them. Remember, the meaning will ultimately live in the person who receives the message, but that doesn't mean that the message sender has no part in crafting that meaning.

From our own research studies as well as many others, we also have many examples of parental memorable messages that the parent likely didn't even know they were sending.[10] An off-handed comment made about someone else in the presence of their child,[11] how they model their own relationships, how they talk about their own bodies[12]—all of these things can become someone else's meaningful socializing message.

We also receive memorable messages from our peers—friends

and romantic partners. Throughout this book, we have shared several of our own. These relationships do not have a presumed direction where one person receives and one person gives the memorable messages, but messages do stem from these relationships all the same. For example, Val recalls years ago ending a longer-term romantic relationship and talking to, at the time, a new friend who would become one of her best friends. Generally relieved but still sad, Val told her friend Dani, "I'm fine, but I'll kind of miss the good morning texts." Dani began texting Val "Good morning!" every morning for the next few months. To this day, Val vividly recalls this as a memorable message. Likely, Dani didn't know she was doing or saying something that Val would still recall 14 years later; she was just being a good friend and a little silly. We remember when people show up for us in big or small ways. But we also remember when someone says something that deeply hurts our feelings or affects our self-concept. We remember when someone makes fun of us, or makes us feel uncertain about who we are.

You never know when something you say or do will become someone else's memorable message, so make intentional choices in your communication to craft the kinds of messages that will be in someone else's "helpful" column, and steer clear of those that could be categorized as hurtful or harmful. To aid in that effort, we will take some time here to discuss what research suggests makes a message more helpful.

As a caveat, as we discussed in Chapter 8, "help" is a personal idea in many ways. Whether or not something helps us in the moment or long-term may vary from person to person and situation to situation. But in a general sense, we will discuss the features of communication that can make a difference and reflect elements of a message that will ultimately help *most* people.

What Makes Advice Useful or Not Useful?

Given that a lot of the memorable messages we may deliver to others (and which we receive ourselves) take the form of advice, we thought it helpful to share some insights from communication scientists[13,14] about what makes advice effective or ineffective. To summarize that research, advice is most effective when:

- It is solicited.
- It attends to face needs.
- It is tailored to the individual by being both feasible and relevant.

Let's talk through each of these.

We are all guilty of sometimes delivering unsolicited advice that no one asked us for. Sometimes, we do this because we feel someone we care about needs to hear something or because we believe we have some insight that will genuinely help another person. We may feel a need to interject before a friend makes what we perceive as a mistake, or to recommend they adopt an action that worked well for us. Admittedly, sometimes we do it because giving advice is fun, and most of us like to do it.

People who are not open to receiving advice typically just reject it, and giving advice when other forms of communication (like emotional support) would be more effective can actually backfire[15] and become someone's unhelpful or harmful memorable message. Many people share stories of people in their lives who try to fix or address problems when all they really want is a hug and an ear. Matching the type of support to the need can be a challenge (especially because in the moment we don't always know exactly what we need), but with practice and intention we can improve.

Advice is only one type of supportive communication. The kinds of support many folks need and want from those in their life are more likely to be emotional or tangible in nature.[16] Emotional support involves helping people feel their feelings, giving them space for their emotional reaction, listening with empathy, and validating their emotions (which is different than validating their behavior—you can disagree with someone's actions and still support them emotionally). Tangible support, sometimes also called instrumental support, is when we actually show up and do something for someone. Helping an overwhelmed friend catch up on their laundry or bringing them a meal, taking your grandparent to an appointment while their car is in the shop, watching your sibling's kids so they can have a break—these are all ways we can tangibly support people. Supportive communication—emotional, tangible, or advice or other informational types of support—all have their place in a relationship. At times, the only way to really help someone involves physically helping. Other times, the only thing that would make a difference is holding someone while they cry. And there are times when the right advice makes all the difference in the world.

Knowing which kind of support to offer someone can be tricky at best. But when in doubt, the person-centered messages we discussed earlier are often emotionally helpful. Person-centered messages focus on emotional validation—specifically, demonstrating that you understand the person's experience of their own stress.[17] Again, emotional validation doesn't mean behavioral validation. You can support someone's emotions without saying that you agree with their behavior or choices. This distinction matters because when people in our life come to us in distress, we often face a temptation to pick apart the situation, their choices, or their behavior.

For example, let's say you have a friend who has an on again-off again relationship with a person you generally don't approve of. Researchers call these cyclical relationships[18]—and your instinct is probably right, they are fraught with uncertainty and often cause a lot of stress. You may not approve of your friend's choices to remain involved with a person who you don't think values them enough, but you can still validate your friend's emotions. The stress and anxiety and sadness they might be experiencing *are* all real because emotions aren't right or wrong, they just are. Accepting the validity of someone's emotional experience frees us from the need to immediately critique their behavior—accepting their experience as their truth, as Brown[19] calls it, is an essential part of empathy. Embracing that empathetic space, we can ask follow-up questions to understand our friend's experience. Being able to articulate that awareness of your friend's emotional stressors can help the friend feel heard and supported.

However, this doesn't mean there is never a place for behavioral feedback. We can both emotionally validate someone and provide feedback with empathy when warranted. As we noted earlier, behavioral feedback is going to be much better received if the person seeks it out—if it's solicited. Unsolicited behavioral feedback will often just be rejected by the message recipient. Advice lands better when we're open to it, but you as the message sender cannot dictate *when* someone will be ready to hear feedback. That said, we receive even unsolicited advice better, and less defensively, when it is paired with emotionally validating messages.

Second, helpful advice attends to face needs. Face, a term you probably have heard before (like saving or losing face), refers to our public-facing image of ourselves. The term was introduced in this context by sociologist Erving Goffman, and later became a component of politeness theory[20]—a social theory that explains the basic features of interaction, how we act toward each other in a way that saves faces and helps maintain politeness. Basically, how do we keep conversations or other social interactions from feeling tense and awkward? Attending to face needs can make advice or any other kind of feedback less likely to elicit a defensive reaction in the message recipient, and more likely to be accepted and ultimately helpful.

We have both positive and negative face needs. Our positive face needs involve the need for inclusion, competence, appreciation, and positive value. We also have negative face needs, which describes our need to be autonomous or feel in control of our time and resources.[21] Advice can be tricky and result in what social scientists describe as *face-threatening communication* because it often implies a person needs assistance of some kind, which is threatening to their positive face needs by suggesting they may not be completely competent or imply otherwise that they are not valued socially, or the advice is telling them what to do, which is threatening to their negative face needs by imposing upon their autonomy.[22] Research demonstrates that advice that neglects face needs will be met with defensiveness or simply rejected altogether. We can take the same principles when thinking about memorable messages, which often contain advice. Effective messages need to attend to those face needs rather than threatening them.

One way to do that is to minimize face threats outright. When feasible, advice that doesn't directly challenge someone's competence, likability, or other elements of their self-concept will be more effective than advice that does. We can do this by avoiding very personal feedback about negative traits or behaviors—framing advice as more about the situation or behaviors rather than the person themselves. For example, rather than telling a friend that they are harming their health by drinking, point out that they may require assistance to quit, highlighting that "I know a lot of my close friends have benefited from attending support groups." This advice is more indirect—you are not telling someone what to do directly or commenting on the person's character, you are highlighting positive regard for others who have followed that advice, and making it less about the specific individual.

Another method is to balance our positive and negative face needs. When giving direct advice, emphasizing the recipient's autonomy ("If you're interested," "I've found this helpful," "It's ultimately up to you") has been found to help prevent negative face threats.[23] Similarly, emphasizing traits that imply care, inclusion, competence, and positive value help preserve positive face needs. For example, if advice contains a critique, balancing that critique with an emphasis on a person's positive traits makes the advice more effective. For example, consider trying to advise a friend that they might want to scale back on a relationship you think is unhealthy. You might start by emphasizing their positive face needs: "You're a really good friend, and I know it comes from a place of kindness, but I'm worried this relationship is putting a lot of stress on you."

Lastly, we should tailor effective advice to the person receiving it. Generic advice can sometimes be helpful. For instance, both of us often tell our students to embrace writing in drafts as an effective writing practice. But when working with students one-on-one, we adapt that generic advice to their specific situation and needs. Tailoring advice means making sure it's both feasible (that the person can actually do the thing you recommend without serious consequences) and that it's actually relevant to them (we often overestimate relevance—assuming that our experiences and situations have more in common with someone else's than they actually do).

Tailored advice means thinking critically about the individual and their circumstances and experiences (and sometimes reminding ourselves to focus on them, rather than ourselves and what we consider relevant). Sometimes, our own experience *is* sincerely relevant. For instance, Val's spouse Sam has an autoimmune disease. About two years ago, our friend and mentee, another brilliant memorable message scholar, Jacqueline, was visiting Val and her spouse in Maine. During that trip, Val's spouse was not doing great—they were ill and struggling. Jacqueline, who has experience with her own autoimmune disease, spent hours of that trip empathetically listening to Sam, commiserating frustrations with the healthcare system and with navigating daily life with emergent symptoms. But she also offered a piece of advice: to ask for a specific blood test that had been helpful to her.

Sam took the advice, and while it did not result in a neat diagnosis, it did lead to the right type of doctor and significant progress. Without that advice, it might have been several more years before Sam found a doctor who could help. Part of why that advice helped is that it was relevant—not all health situations are comparable, but after hours of listening to Sam talk about their experience and symptoms, Jacqueline felt like it was (and it was). The other reason that this advice landed well was because in several hours of conversation, that was the only advice Jacqueline really gave. The rest of the conversation included listening empathetically and validating the reasonably frustrating experiences. Having felt like they had been heard, Sam was much more willing to accept the advice from a friend. To this date, Sam tells Val this was one of the most useful pieces of advice they received (among many, many not so useful pieces of advice) related to their chronic health problems.

Features of Helpful Memorable Messages from the Research

Earlier, we asked you to consider what features of the memorable messages you have received throughout your life you would generally classify as helpful and distill it into a declarative statement about what makes a message helpful. Here, we will talk briefly about some of the characteristics of helpful memorable messages throughout the research literature—that is, what people generally find helpful in their own memorable messages. Earlier in the book, we discuss these ideas in more detail, but to follow our own recommendations and distill these findings into a declarative statement: Memorable messages are generally most helpful when they are positive, tailored to the individual, contain comprehensive information, come from people we care about during important life moments, and demonstrate empathy. As we conclude this book, we'll summarize some of those features here.

On positivity, we know from memorable message research that people generally prefer messages that are more positive than negative. That said, expecting all communication in every context to reflect positive ideas is unrealistic at best. Not everything is positive. Sometimes things suck, and putting a positive spin on something distressing can backfire and make people feel worse. When thinking about the messages you send others, positive messages are more helpful generally. Reminding ourselves to generally be positive is good advice—but that doesn't mean there aren't appropriate exceptions to that rule. It also doesn't mean, if a message doesn't immediately make us feel positive, that the message is bad, harmful, or not useful. Sometimes we need messages that challenge us or help us embrace and work through uncomfortable feelings like grief or anger.

Comprehensive messages, which contain nuanced and complete information rather than overly simplistic information, take practice and intention. We're not all experts in everything, and that's okay—especially for parents. Research actually shows that when it comes to topics like health, sex, and relationships, young people care less about receiving detailed medical information from their parents, and more about receiving balanced messages that avoid shaming them, that acknowledge the role of parents as a gatekeeper for health access (such as explicitly saying that a parent will bring their child to a doctor, buy them desired period products, or give them a ride somewhere), and share both good and bad personal experiences.[24,25,26] Comprehensive messages tend to reflect more dialogue than individual, discrete messages. That is, they feel less like one brief, memorable phrase, and more like a series of ongoing conversations that we find memorable and impactful.

And lastly, effective messages are empathetic. We have noted this repeatedly throughout this book. Empathy is easier said than done—for some people, it comes naturally, but for others, it has to be intentional, a choice that we make to feel with others and keep our hearts open to theirs. Like most communication behaviors, empathy can be learned. If you feel your messages sometimes lack empathy, or could just stand to be a little more empathetic, remembering to let people feel their feelings and to accept their feelings as their truth helps ground empathetic communication and enables us to craft more empathetic verbal responses.[27] But empathy is also nonverbal—making sure someone feels you are listening to them (put your phone away, face them, nod, ask follow-up questions). Feeling truly heard in an important moment can become someone's memorable message.

With this in mind, take some space here to reflect on messages you have given other people that you think (or hope) might become memorable to them. What message did you intend for them to receive and why?

If you could go back in time, would you adjust the message or the way in which you delivered it? Consider if the message contained advice—and if, based on the circumstances of that conversation, the advice was appropriate. Did it attend to the person's face needs? Was it solicited? Was it tailored to the individual? If the message did not contain advice, was it positive, comprehensive, and empathetic? If not, how might you revise the message to reflect these more helpful characteristics?

Although a lot of the research we discussed in this chapter and throughout the book focuses on parents as a common source of messages, you do not need to be a parent in order to send memorable messages. We recall messages from anyone important in our lives. For every friend, romantic partner, colleague, even neighbor, you could be a potential source of memorable messages.

Before ending with some of our concluding thoughts, we suggest taking another moment to reflect on your own goals as a communicator. Consider the following:

- Overall, how do you feel about the messages you send to others?
- In what ways do the messages you send offer comfort, assistance, or value to the people you care about?
- In what ways do you want to adjust your behavior to make your messages more memorable or more helpful?

Concluding Thoughts

In many ways, memorable messages underlie the elements of ourselves, our relationships, and our lives that give them meaning. Taking the time to understand your own, working on getting the most out of them, and thinking seriously about the messages you give others are important tasks. But we also know that these tasks are not easy for many. It takes time, introspection, and vulnerability to engage with this level of self-work. Digging deep into ourselves and our memories like this can feel overwhelming.

We want to take this space to express our appreciation to you for making your way through this book, learning about memorable messages, and doing the work on your own. We invite you to continue this work, using the prompts we provide here to work through messages you have received throughout your life and will continue to receive into the future. Take the time to be intentional about the messages you send and receive and the scripts you generate from them.

Finally, we want to conclude this book with how we started it. Remember, we are not passive recipients of the communication we receive from the world around us. Communication variables do in fact predict a lot of the positive outcomes of most personal and professional relationships. But in order for communication to offer a solution to many of our social and interpersonal challenges, we must take an active role in the process. We must think critically about the messages we send and receive, and break out of autopilot to more mindfully interact with others and with ourselves.

We hope you leave this book with tools to step into that

process and take ownership over the messages you share and receive. We can't control the messages shared with us, but we can control what we do with them. Endorsing a memorable message is a choice, and if you're unsatisfied with yours, it's time to make another one.

Chapter Notes

Preface

1. Knapp, M.L., C. Stohl, and K.K. Reardon. 1981. "'Memorable' Messages." *Journal of Communication*, 31(4), 27–41. https://doi.org/10.1111/j.1460-2466.1981.tb00448.x.

Chapter 1

1. Akhlaq, A., N.I. Malik, and N.A. Khan. 2013. "Family Communication and Family System as the Predictors of Family Satisfaction in Adolescents." *Science Journal of Psychology.* http://doi.org/10.7237/sjpsych/258.

2. Szcześniak, M., I. Bajkowska, A. Czaprowska, and A. Sileńska. 2022. "Adolescents' Self-Esteem and Life Satisfaction: Communication with Peers as a Mediator." *International Journal of Environmental Research and Public Health*, 19(7), 3777. https://doi.org/10.3390/ijerph19073777.

3. Eğeci, İ. S., and T. Gençöz. 2006. "Factors Associated with Relationship Satisfaction: Importance of Communication Skills." *Contemporary Family Therapy*, 28, 383–391. https://doi.org/10.1007/s10591-006-9010-2

4. Abugre, J.B. 2011. "Appraising the Impact of Organizational Communication on Worker Satisfaction in Organizational Workplace." *Problems of Management in the 21st Century*, 1(1), 7–15. https://www.ceeol.com/search/article-detail?id=1034475.

5. Wanzer, M.B., M. Booth-Butterfield, and K. Gruber. 2004. "Perceptions of Health Care Providers' Communication: Relationships Between Patient-Centered Communication and Satisfaction." *Health Communication*, 16(3), 363–384. https://doi.org/10.1207/S15327027HC1603_6.

6. Honeycutt, J.M., C.M. Mapp, K.A. Knasser, and J.M. Banner. 2014. "Intrapersonal Communication and Imagined Interactions." In *An Integrated Approach to Communication Theory and Research*, edited by D.W. Stacks and M.B. Salwen. Routledge.

7. Knapp, M. L., C. Stohl, and K.K. Reardon. 1981. "'Memorable' Messages." *Journal of Communication*, 31(4), 27–41. https://doi.org/10.1111/j.1460-2466.1981.tb00448.x.

8. Jensen, A., and S. Trenholm. 1995. *Interpersonal Communication.* Oxford University Press.

9. Marshall, D., J. Yeargain, J. Pulliam, S. Kim, and V. VanNest. 2022. *It's About Them: Public Speaking in the 21st Century.* Louis Pressbooks.

10. Greenwell, M.R. 2019. "Memorable Messages from Family Members About Mental Health: Young Adult Perceptions of Relational Closeness, Message Satisfaction, and Clinical Help-Seeking Attitudes." *Health Communication*, 34(6), 652–660. https://doi.org/10.1080/10410236.2018.1431021.

11. Cooke-Jackson, A., and V. Rubinsky. 2018. "Deeply Rooted in Memories: Toward a Comprehensive Overview of 30 Years of Memorable Message Literature." *Health Communication*, 33(4), 409–422. https://doi.org/10.1080/10410236.2016.1278491.

12. Cooke-Jackson and Rubinsky 2018. "Deeply Rooted in Memories."

13. Cooke-Jackson, A., and V. Rubinsky.

2023. "Extending the Roots of Memorable Messages: A Comprehensive Review and Forecast of Memorable Message Literature and Theory." *Health Communication*, 38(12), 2676–2686. https://doi.org/10.1080/10410236.2022.2105620.

14. Majerus, S. 2013. "Language Repetition and Short-Term Memory: An Integrative Framework." *Frontiers in Human Neuroscience*, 7, 357. https://doi.org/10.3389/fnhum.2013.00357.

15. DeGroot, J.M. 2024. "'You Think This Is Hard? Just Wait...': Memorable Messages in Motherhood." *Western Journal of Communication*, 88(2), 418–435. https://doi.org/10.1080/10570314.2023.2219241.

16. Brown, N R., and L.T. Wingate. 2024. "The Influence of Memorable Message Receipt on Dietary and Exercise Behavior among Self-Identified Black Women." In *Emergent Health Communication Scholarship from and about African American, Latino/a/x, and American Indian/Alaskan Native Peoples*, edited by A. Cooke-Jackson. Routledge.

17. Nazione et al. 2011. "Memorable Messages for Navigating College Life." *Journal of Applied Communication Research*, 39(2). https://doi.org/10.1080/00909882.2011.556138.

18. Knapp, Stohl, and Reardon. "'Memorable' Messages."

19. Dallimore, E.J. 2003. "Memorable Messages as Discursive Formations: The Gendered Socialization of New University Faculty." *Women's Studies in Communication*, 26(2), 214–265. https://doi.org/10.1080/07491409.2003.10162460.

20. Cranmer, G.A. 2017. "A Communicative Approach to Sport Socialization: The Functions of Memorable Messages in Division-I Student-Athletes' Socialization." *International Journal of Sport Communication*, 10(2), 233–257. https://doi.org/10.1123/IJSC.2017-0031.

21. Dallimore. "Memorable Messages as Discursive Formations."

22. Kellas, J.K. 2010. "Transmitting Relational Worldviews: The Relationship between Mother–Daughter Memorable Messages and Adult Daughters' Romantic Relational Schemata." *Communication Quarterly*, 58(4), 458–479. https://doi.org/10.1080/01463373.2010.525700.

23. Stohl, C. 1986. "The Role of Memorable Messages in the Process of Organizational Socialization." *Communication Quarterly*, 34(3), 231–249. https://doi.org/10.1080/01463378609369638.

Chapter 2

1. Kukushkin, N.V., T. Tabassum, and T.J. Carew. 2022. "Precise Timing of ERK Phosphorylation/ Dephosphorylation Determines the Outcome of Trial Repetition During Long-Term Memory Formation." *Proceedings of the National Academy of Sciences*, 119(40), e2210478119. https://doi.org/10.1073/pnas.2210478119.

2. Hintzman, D.L. 2010. "How Does Repetition Affect Memory? Evidence from Judgments of Recency." *Memory and Cognition*, 38, 102–115. http://doi.org/10.3758/MC.38.1.102.

3. Cooke-Jackson and Rubinsky 2023. "Extending the Roots of Memorable Messages."

4. Rubinsky, V., and A. Cooke-Jackson. 2017. "'Where is the love?' Expanding and Theorizing with LGBTQ Memorable Messages of Sex and Sexuality." *Health Communication*, 32(12), 1472–1480. https://doi.org/10.1080/10410236.2016.1230809.

5. Dailey, S.L., and L. Browning. 2014. "Retelling Stories in Organizations: Understanding the Functions of Narrative Repetition." *Academy of Management Review*, 39(1), 22–43. https://doi.org/10.5465/amr.2011.0329.

6. Rossi, N.E. 2010. "'Coming Out' Stories of Gay and Lesbian Young Adults." *Journal of Homosexuality*, 57(9), 1174–1191. https://doi.org/10.1080/00918369.2010.508330.

7. Haltom, T.M., and S. Ratcliff. 2021. "Effects of Sex, Race, and Education on the Timing of Coming Out Among Lesbian, Gay, and Bisexual Adults in the U.S." *Archives of Sexual Behavior*, 50, 1107–1120. http://doi.org/10.1007/s10508-020-01776-x.

8. Rubinsky, V., A.M. Hosek, and N. Hudak. 2019. "'It's better to be depressed skinny than happy fat': College Women's Memorable Body Messages and Their Impact on Body Image, Self-Esteem, and Rape Myth Acceptance." *Health*

Communication, 34(13), 1555–1563. https://doi.org/10.1080/10410236.2018.1504659.

9. Rounsefell, K., S. Gibson, S. McLean, M. Blair, A. Molenaar, L. Brennan, H. Truby, and T.A. McCaffrey. 2020. "Social Media, Body Image and Food Choices in Healthy Young Adults: A Mixed Methods Systematic Review." *Nutrition and Dietetics*, 77(1), 19–40. https://doi.org/10.1111/1747-0080.12581.

10. Barbeau, K., N. Carbonneau, and L. Pelletier. 2022. "Family Members and Peers' Negative and Positive Body Talk: How They Relate to Adolescent Girls' Body Talk and Eating Disorder Attitudes." *Body Image*, 40, 213–224. https://doi.org/10.1016/j.bodyim.2021.12.010.

11. Hirst, W., and E.A. Phelps. 2016. "Flashbulb Memories." *Current Directions in Psychological Science*, 25(1), 36–41. https://doi.org/10.1177/0963721415622487.

12. Aragón, A., A. Cooke-Jackson, J. Oliva, P. Lainez, M. Huerta, M. Roldán, and V. Rubinsky. 2023. "Setting the Agenda: Latina/x Tri-Generational Family Communication About Reproductive and Sexual Health Toward Wellbeing." *Journal of Family Communication*, 23(2), 171–178. https://doi.org/10.1080/15267431.2023.2186883.

Chapter 3

1. Kuang, K., Z. Tian, S.R. Wilson, and P.M. Buzzanell. 2023. "Memorable Messages as Anticipatory Resilience: Examining Associations Among Memorable Messages, Communication Resilience Processes, and Mental Health." *Health Communication*, 38(6), 1136–1145. https://doi.org/10.1080/10410236.2021.1993585.

2. Southwick, S. M., G.A. Bonanno, A.S. Masten, C. Panter-Brick, and R. Yehuda. 2014. "Resilience Definitions, Theory, and Challenges: Interdisciplinary Perspectives." *European Journal of Psychotraumatology*, 5(1), 25338. http://doi.org/10.3402/ejpt.v5.25338@zept20.2014.5.issue-s4.

3. Lucas, K., and P.M. Buzzanell. 2012. "Memorable Messages of Hard Times: Constructing Short- and Long-Term Resiliencies Through Family Communication." *Journal of Family Communication*, 12(3), 189–208. https://doi.org/10.1080/15267431.2012.687196.

4. Cooke-Jackson and Rubinsky 2023. "Extending the Roots of Memorable Messages."

5. Franiuk, R., D. Cohen, and E.M. Pomerantz. 2002. "Implicit Theories of Relationships: Implications for Relationship Satisfaction and Longevity." *Personal Relationships*, 9(4), 345–367. https://doi.org/10.1111/1475-6811.09401.

Chapter 4

1. Watzlawick, P., J. Beavin, and D. Jackson. 2008. "Some Tentative Axioms of Communication." In *Communication Theory*, edited by C.D. Mortensen. Routledge.

2. Stohl, C. 1986. "The Role of Memorable Messages in the Process of Organizational Socialization." *Communication Quarterly*, 34(3), 231–249. https://doi.org/10.1080/01463378609369638.

3. CDC. 2025. "Intimate Partner Violence." https://www.cdc.gov/intimate-partner-violence/about/index.html.

4. Plaks, J.E. 2017. "Implicit Theories: Assumptions that Shape Social and Moral Cognition." *Advances in Experimental Social Psychology*, 56, 259–310. https://doi.org/10.1016/bs.aesp.2017.02.003.

5. Heisler, J.M. 2014. "They Need to Sow Their Wild Oats: Mothers' Recalled Memorable Messages to Their Emerging Adult Children Regarding Sexuality and Dating." *Emerging Adulthood*, 2(4), 280–293. https://doi.org/10.1177/2167696814550196.

6. Astle, S., K. Anders, A. Shigeto, and K. Rodriguez. 2023. "College Women's Memorable Sexual Messages from Mothers, Fathers, Friends/Peers, and Online Media: A Mixed-Methods Latent Class Analysis." *Emerging Adulthood*, 11(1), 133–147. https://doi.org/10.1177/2167696822109845.

7. Rubinsky, V., and A. Cooke-Jackson. 2017. "'Tell me something other than to use a condom and sex is scary': Memorable Messages Women and Gender Minorities Wish for and Recall About Sexual Health." *Women's Studies in Communication*, 40(4), 379–400. https://doi.org/10.1080/07491409.2017.1368761.

Chapter 5

1. Mineo, L. 2017. "Good Genes are Nice, but Joy Is Better." *Harvard University News.* https://news.harvard.edu/gazette/story/2017/04/over-nearly-80-years-harvard-study-has-been-showing-how-to-live-a-healthy-and-happy-life/.

2. Righetti, F., R. Faure, G. Zoppolat, A. Meltzer, and J. McNulty. 2022. "Factors that Contribute to the Maintenance or Decline of Relationship Satisfaction." *Nature Reviews Psychology,* 1(3), 161–173. https://www.nature.com/articles/s44159-022-00026-2.

3. Holman, A., and J. Koenig Kellas. 2018. "'Say something instead of nothing': Adolescents' Perceptions of Memorable Conversations About Sex-Related Topics with Their Parents." *Communication Monographs,* 85(3), 357–379. https://doi.org/10.1080/03637751.2018.1426870.

4. Hosek, A.M., V. Rubinsky, N. Hudak, S. Davari Zanjani, and S. Sanburg. 2021. "Exploring the Type and Impact of Memorable Hate Messages and Identity Salience on Self-Esteem, Relational Outcomes, and Intergroup Biases." *Journal of Intercultural Communication Research,* 50(2), 103–121. https://doi.org/10.1080/17475759.2021.1888147.

5. Flood-Grady, E., S.C. Starcher, and G.L. Bergquist. 2023. "Parental Memorable Messages About Depression: Implications for Perceived Support, Stigma, Relational Satisfaction, and Treatment-Seeking among Young Adults with Depression." *Health Communication,* 38(1), 11–20. https://doi.org/10.1080/10410236.2021.1926108

6. Vangelisti, A. L., and A.D. Hampel. 2010. "Hurtful Communication: Current Research and Future Directions." In *New Directions in Interpersonal Communication Research,* edited by S. Smith and S.R. Wilson. Sage.

7. O'Hara, S., and A. Cooke-Jackson. 2023. "Stokes, Thomas 'Ty.'" Oxford African American Studies Center. https://oxfordaasc.com/display/10.1093/acref/9780195301731.001.0001/acref-9780195301731-e-80456.

8. Kellas 2010. "Transmitting Relational Worldviews."

9. Lucas and Buzzanell 2012. "Memorable Messages of Hard Times."

10. Aragón, Cooke-Jackson, Oliva, Lainez, Huerta, Roldán, and Rubinsky 2023. "Setting the agenda."

11. Aragón, A., and A. Cooke-Jackson. 2021. "The Sex Talk Was Taboo... So Was Wearing a Tampon." In *Communicating Intimate Health,* edited by A. Cooke-Jackson and V. Rubinsky. Rowman and Littlefield.

12. Koenig Kellas, J., and A.R. Trees. 2021. "Family Stories and Storytelling: Windows into the Family Soul." In *The Routledge Handbook of Family Communication,* edited by J. Koenig Kellas and A.R. Trees. Routledge.

13. Kellas 2010. "Transmitting Relational Worldviews."

14. Rubinsky and Cooke-Jackson 2017. "'Where is the love?'"

15. Fitzpatrick, M.A. 1984. "A Typological Approach to Marital Interaction: Recent Theory and Research." *Advances in Experimental Social Psychology,* 18, 1–47. https://doi.org/10.1016/S0065-2601(08)60141-0.

16. Kellas 2010. "Transmitting Relational Worldviews."

17. Fitzpatrick 1984. "A Typological Approach to Marital Interaction."

18. Kellas 2010. "Transmitting Relational Worldviews."

Chapter 6

1. Knapp, Stohl, and Reardon. "'Memorable' Messages."

2. Yeung, K.T., and J.L. Martin. 2003. "The Looking Glass Self: An Empirical Test and Elaboration." *Social Forces,* 81(3), 843–879. https://doi.org/10.1353/sof.2003.0048.

3. Hogg, M.A. 2016. "Social Identity Theory." In *Understanding Peace and Conflict Through Social Identity Theory,* edited by S. McKeown, R. Haji, and N. Ferguson. Springer International Publishing.

4. Park, L.E., and J. Crocker. 2005. "Interpersonal Consequences of Seeking Self-Esteem." *Personality and Social Psychology Bulletin,* 31(11), 1587–1598. https://doi.org/10.1177/0146167205277206.

5. Cooke-Jackson, A., and V. Rubinsky. 2021. "Theory of Memorable Messages." In *Communicating Intimate Health,*

edited by A. Cooke-Jackson and V. Rubinsky. Rowman and Littlefield.

6. Smith, S.W., J. Butler Ellis, and H.J. Yoo. 2001. "Memorable Messages as Guides to Self-Assessment of Behavior: The Role of Instrumental Values." *Communication Monographs*, 68(4), 325–339. https://doi.org/10.1080/03637750128072.

7. Rubinsky, Hosek, and Hudak 2019. "'It's better to be depressed skinny than happy fat.'"

8. Hosek, Rubinsky, Hudak, Davari Zanjani, and Sanburg 2021. "Exploring the Type and Impact of Memorable Hate Messages and Identity Salience."

9. Hosek, A.M., C. Densmore, V. Rubinsky, C. Waldbuesser, M. Rizzo, and J.M. Cueller. 2024. "'Math is for life. We use it every day': Examining Memorable Messages Parents Give to Their Children About Math Education and Predictors of Their Own Math Self-Anxiety, Math Self-Concept, and Math Self-Efficacy." *Atlantic Journal of Communication*, 1–14. https://doi.org/10.1080/15456870.2024.2314019.

10. Kernis, M H., and B.M. Goldman. 2013. "Assessing Stability of Self-Esteem and Contingent Self-Esteem." In *Self-Esteem Issues and Answers*, edited by M.H. Kernis. Psychology Press.

11. Orth, U., and R.W. Robins. 2014. "The Development of Self-Esteem." *Current Directions in Psychological Science*, 23(5), 381–387. https://doi.org/10.1177/0963721414547414.

12. Hosek, Densmore, Rubinsky, Waldbuesser, Rizzo, and Cueller 2024. "'Math is for life. We use it every day.'"

13. Knapp, Stohl, and Reardon. "'Memorable' Messages."

14. Martiny, S.E., and M. Rubin. 2016. "Towards a Clearer Understanding of Social Identity Theory's Self-Esteem Hypothesis." In *Understanding Peace and Conflict Through Social Identity Theory*, edited by S. McKeown, R. Haji, and N. Ferguson. Springer International Publishing.

15. Minniear, M.J., T. Pierce, and J. Morrison. 2023. "Raising Black Daughters: Using Intersectionality and Memorable Messages to Understand Parental Gendered Racial Socialization." *Journal of Family Communication*, 23(3–4), 226–240. https://doi.org/10.1080/15267431.2023.2239206.

16. Minniear, Pierce, and Morrison 2023. "Raising Black Daughters."

17. Collins, P.H., and S. Bilge. 2020. *Intersectionality*. John Wiley and Sons.

18. McLean, K. C., M. Pasupathi, and M. Syed. 2023. "Cognitive Scripts and Narrative Identity Are Shaped by Structures of Power." *Trends in Cognitive Sciences*, 27(9), 805–813. https://www.cell.com/trends/cognitive-sciences/abstract/S1364-6613(23)00068-2.

19. Heisler, J. M., and J.B. Ellis. 2008. "Motherhood and the Construction of 'Mommy Identity': Messages About Motherhood and Face Negotiation." *Communication Quarterly*, 56(4), 445–467. https://doi.org/10.1080/01463370802448246.

20. DeGroot 2024. "'You Think This Is Hard? Just Wait…'"

21. Kuang, Tian, Wilson, and Buzzanell 2023. "Memorable Messages as Anticipatory Resilience."

22. Horstman, H. K., A. Pedro, T. Goldschmidt, O. Watson, and M. Butauski, M. 2023. "Exploring Resilience and Communicated Narrative Sense-Making in South Africans' Stories of Apartheid." *International Journal of Communication*, 17, 19. https://ijoc.org/index.php/ijoc/article/view/19464.

Chapter 7

1. Smith, S., and J. Butler Ellis. 2001. "Memorable Messages as Guides to Self-Assessment of Behavior: An Initial Investigation." *Communication Monographs*, 68(2), 154–168. https://doi.org/10.1080/03637750128058.

2. Smith, Butler Ellis, and Yoo 2001. "Memorable Messages as Guides to Self-Assessment of Behavior."

3. Ellis, J.B., and S.W. Smith. 2004. "Memorable Messages as Guides to Self-Assessment of Behavior: A Replication and Extension Diary Study." *Communication Monographs*, 71(1), 97–119. https://doi.org/10.1080/03634520410001691456.

4. Smith, Butler Ellis, and Yoo 2001. "Memorable Messages as Guides to Self-Assessment of Behavior."

5. McGrath, A. 2017. "Dealing with Dissonance: A Review of Cognitive Dissonance Reduction." *Social and Personality*

Psychology Compass, 11(12), e12362. https://doi.org/10.1111/spc3.12362.

6. Voorhees, H. L., J. Koenig Kellas, A.L. Palmer-Wackerly, J.N. Gunning, J.S. Marsh, and J. Baker, J. 2024. "Making Sense of Memorable Messages About Infertility: Examining Message Valence by Theme and Sender." *Health Communication*, 39(10), 2053–2065. https://doi.org/10.1080/10410236.2023.2254928.

7. Rubinsky, Hosek, and Hudak 2019. "'It's better to be depressed skinny than happy fat.'"

8. Gettings, P.E., and K. Kuang. 2024. "Examining the Role of Memorable Messages in the Process of Communication about Aging." *Health Communication, 39*(10), 2174–2185. https://doi.org/10.1080/10410236.2023.2258307.

9. Gettings and Kuang 2024. "Examining the Role of Memorable Messages in the Process of Communication About Aging."

10. Kuang, Tian, Wilson, and Buzzanell 2023. "Memorable Messages as Anticipatory Resilience."

11. Kellas, J.K., T. Morgan, C. Taladay, M. Minton, J. Forte, and E. Husmann. 2020. "Narrative Connection: Applying CNSM Theory's Translational Storytelling Heuristic." *Journal of Family Communication*, 20(4), 360–376. https://doi.org/10.1080/15267431.2020.1826485.

12. Cooke-Jackson and Rubinsky 2023. "Extending the Roots of Memorable Messages."

13. Rubinsky, V., J.N. Gunning, and A. Cooke-Jackson. 2020. "'I thought I was dying':(Un) Supportive Communication Surrounding Early Menstruation Experiences." *Health Communication*, 35(2), 242–252. https://doi.org/10.1080/10410236.2018.1548337.

Chapter 8

1. Vaish, A., T. Grossmann, and A. Woodward. 2008. "Not All Emotions Are Created Equal: The Negativity Bias in Social-Emotional Development." *Psychological Bulletin*, 134(3), 383. https://psycnet.apa.org/buy/2008-04614-002.

2. Rubinsky, Gunning, and Cooke-Jackson 2020. "'I thought I was dying.'"

3. LeBlanc, S.S. 2024. "Breaking the Cycle: Memorable Messages of "Grin 'n' Bear It" and Silence in Menarche Narrative Recall." *Qualitative Research in Medicine and Healthcare*, 8(2), 12239. http://doi.org/10.4081/qrmh.2024.12239.

4. Kastrinos, A., C.L. Fisher, D. Bagautdinova, G. Taylor III, M. Behrens, M., and C.L. Bylund. 2024. "Applications of Turning Point Analysis in Behavioral Medicine Research: A Systematic Scoping Review." *Social Science and Medicine*, 116987. https://doi.org/10.1016/j.socscimed.2024.116987.

Chapter 9

1. Demir, M. 2010. "Close Relationships and Happiness Among Emerging Adults." *Journal of Happiness Studies*, 11, 293–313. http://doi.org/10.1007/s10902-009-9141-x.

2. Gardiner, G., K. Sauerberger, D. Lee, and D. Funder, D. 2022. "What Happy People Do: The Behavioral Correlates of Happiness in Everyday Situations." *Journal of Research in Personality*, 99, 104236. https://doi.org/10.1016/j.jrp.2022.104236.

3. Lu, L. 1999. "Personal or Environmental Causes of Happiness: A Longitudinal Analysis." *The Journal of Social Psychology*, 139(1), 79–90. https://doi.org/10.1080/00224549909598363.

4. Gupta, S.D., and D. Kumar. 2010. "Psychological Correlates of Happiness." *Indian Journal of Social Science Researches*, 7(1), 60–64.

5. Suardi, A., I. Sotgiu, T. Costa, F. Cauda, and M. Rusconi. 2016. "The Neural Correlates of Happiness: A Review of PET and fMRI Studies Using Autobiographical Recall Methods." *Cognitive, Affective, and Behavioral Neuroscience*, 16, 383–392. https://doi.org/10.3758/s13415-016-0414-7.

6. Shilton, A.C. 2019. "You Accomplished Something Great. So Now What?" *New York Times*. https://www.nytimes.com/2019/05/28/smarter-living/you-accomplished-something-great-so-now-what.html.

7. Rubinsky and Cooke-Jackson. "'Tell me something other than to use a condom and sex is scary.'"

8. Brown, N.R., and L.A. Davis. 2023. "Memorable Diet and Exercise Messages

Recalled by Black Women." *Southern Communication Journal*, 88(5), 428–440. https://doi.org/10.1080/1041794X.2023.2228756.

9. Basinger, E.D., M.M. Quinlan, and M. Rawlings. 2023. "Memorable Messages About Fat Bodies Before, During, and After Pregnancy." *Health Communication*, 38(13), 3069–3079. https://doi.org/10.1080/10410236.2022.2131982.

10. Russell, J., and S.W. Smith. 2017. "An Examination of Weight-Associated Memorable Messages, Sources, and Outcomes." *Atlantic Journal of Communication*, 25(5), 263–279. https://doi.org/10.1080/15456870.2017.1377045.

11. Hall, K.D., and S. Kahan. 2018. "Maintenance of Lost Weight and Long-Term Management of Obesity." *The Medical Clinics of North America*, 102(1), 183–197. https://doi.org/10.1016/j.mcna.2017.08.012.

12. Greenhalgh, S. 2016. "Disordered Eating/Eating Disorder: Hidden Perils of the Nation's Fight against Fat." *Medical Anthropology Quarterly*, 30(4), 545–562. https://doi.org/10.1111/maq.12257.

13. Jordan, E. 2023. "'If you don't lose weight, the government will take you away': An Analysis of Memorable Messages and Eating Disorders in the LGBTQ+ Community." *Health Communication*, 38(13), 2925–2935. https://doi.org/10.1080/10410236.2022.2126695.

14. Manusov, V., and B. Spitzberg. 2008. "Attribution Theory." In *Engaging Theories in Interpersonal Communication: Multiple perspectives*, edited by L.A. Baxter and D.O. Braithwaiet. Sage.

15. Rubinsky and Cooke-Jackson. "'Tell me something other than to use a condom and sex is scary.'"

16. Rubinsky and Cooke-Jackson. "'Tell me something other than to use a condom and sex is scary.'"

Chapter 10

1. Cooper, A. 2024. "All There Is with Anderson Cooper: Andrew Garfield's Grief." https://www.cnn.com/audio/podcasts/all-there-is-with-anderson-cooper/episodes/e92bef56-387b-11ef-8459-83008f425ae3.

2. DeGroot, J.M., and H.J. Carmack. 2022. "'I know they meant well…': Helpful and Hurtful Memorable Messages During Mourning." *Journal of Loss and Trauma*, 27(5), 418–430. https://doi.org/10.1080/15325024.2021.1994224.

3. High, A.C., and J.P. Dillard. 2012. "A Review and Meta-Analysis of Person-Centered Messages and Social Support Outcomes." *Communication Studies*, 63(1), 99–118. https://doi.org/10.1080/10510974.2011.598208.

4. Jones, S.M., G.D. Bodie, and A.F. Koerner. 2017. "Connections between Family Communication Patterns, Person-Centered Message Evaluations, and Emotion Regulation Strategies." *Human Communication Research*, 43(2), 237–255. https://doi.org/10.1111/hcre.12103.

5. Kuang, Tian, Wilson, and Buzzanell 2023. "Memorable Messages as Anticipatory Resilience."

6. High and Dillard 2012. "A Review and Meta-Analysis of Person-Centered Messages and Social Support Outcomes."

7. High and Dillard 2012. "A Review and Meta-Analysis of Person-Centered Messages and Social Support Outcomes."

8. Tian, X., Y. Li, and D.H. Solomon. 2024. "How Do Qualities of Supportive Conversations Affect Heart Rate Variability During Conversations about the Death of a Parent?" *Health Communication*, 39(10), 1998–2013. https://doi.org/10.1080/10410236.2023.2252639.

9. Brown, B. "Empathy v. Sympathy." https://www.youtube.com/watch?v=1Evwgu369Jw.

10. Stevens, S.K., R. Brustad, L. Gilbert, B. Houge, T. Milbrandt, K. Munson, K., and M.A. Siddiqui. 2020. "The Use of Empathic Communication During the Covid-19 Outbreak." *Journal of Patient Experience*, 7(5), 648–652. https://doi.org/10.1177/23743735209626.

11. Brown, B. "Empathy v. Sympathy."

12. Brown, B. "Empathy v. Sympathy."

13. Bargh, J.A., and E.L. Williams. 2006. "The Automaticity of Social Life." *Current Directions in Psychological Science*, 15(1), 1–4.

14. Garcia, T., and P.R. Pintrich. 2023. "Regulating Motivation and Cognition in the Classroom: The Role of Self-Schemas and Self-Regulatory Strategies." In *Self-Regulation of Learning and*

Performance, edited by D.H. Schunk and B.J. Zimmerman. Routledge.

15. Seow, T.X., M. Rouault, C.M. Gillan, and S.M. Fleming. 2021. "How Local and Global Metacognition Shape Mental Health." *Biological Psychiatry*, 90(7), 436–446. https://doi.org/10.1016/j.biopsych.2021.05.013.

16. Costos, D., R. Ackerman, and L. Paradis. 2002. "Recollections of Menarche: Communication between Mothers and Daughters Regarding Menstruation." *Sex Roles*, 46, 49–59. http://doi.org/10.1023/A:1016037618567.

17. Rubinsky, Gunning, and Cooke-Jackson 2020. "'I thought I was dying.'"

18. Kissling, E.A. 1996. "'That's just a basic teen-age rule': Girls' Linguistic Strategies for Managing the Menstrual Communication Taboo." *Journal of Applied Communication Research*, 292–309. https://doi.org/10.1080/00909889609365458.

19. Rubinsky, V., and A. Cooke-Jackson. 2018. "Sex as an Intergroup Arena: How Women and Gender Minorities Conceptualize Sex, Sexuality, and Sexual Health." *Communication Studies*, 69(2), 213–234. https://doi.org/10.1080/10510974.2018.1437549.

20. Basinger, E.D., and M.M. Quinlan. 2024. "'She didn't think fat women deserved to have children': Memorable Messages from Healthcare Providers in the Context of Fat Pregnancy." *Women's Reproductive Health*, 11(1), 33–47. https://doi.org/10.1080/23293691.2023.2174823.

21. Gunning, J.N., A. Cooke-Jackson, and V. Rubinsky. 2023. "Sex, Blood, and Redefining 'Womanhood': Intervening Early Intimate Health Messages." In *Sex Education Research*, edited by B. Taverner. Routledge.

Chapter 11

1. Ramos Salazar, L. 2022. "The Mediating Effect of Mindfulness and Self-Compassion on Leaders' Communication Competence and Job Satisfaction." *Journal of Communication Management*, 26(1), 39–57. https://doi.org/10.1108/JCOM-07-2021-0074.

2. Cooke-Jackson and Rubinsky 2023. "Extending the Roots of Memorable Messages."

3. Medved, C.E., S.M. Brogan, A.M. McClanahan, J.F. Morris, and G.J. Shepherd. 2006. "Family and Work Socializing Communication: Messages, Gender, and Ideological Implications." *The Journal of Family Communication*, 6(3), 161–180. https://doi.org/10.1207/s15327698jfc0603_1.

4. Kranstuber, H., K. Carr, and A.M. Hosek. 2012. "'If you can dream it, you can achieve it': Parent Memorable Messages as Indicators of College Student Success." *Communication Education*, 61(1), 44–66. https://doi.org/10.1080/03634523.2011.620617.

5. Scarduzio, J.A., K. Real, A. Slone, and Z. Henning. 2018. "Vocational Anticipatory Socialization, Self-Determination Theory, and Meaningful Work: Parents' and Children's Recollection of Memorable Messages About Work." *Management Communication Quarterly*, 32(3), 431–461. https://doi.org/10.1177/0893318918768711.

6. Waldron, V.R., D. Kloeber, C. Goman, N. Piemonte, and J. Danaher. 2014. "How Parents Communicate Right and Wrong: A Study of Memorable Moral Messages Recalled by Emerging Adults." *Journal of Family Communication*, *14*(4), 374–397. https://doi.org/10.1080/15267431.2014.946032.

7. Di Pietro, M.L., D. Zaçe, A. Orfino, F.R. Di Raimo, A. Poscia, E. De Matteis, and M. Genuardi, M. 2021. "Intrafamilial Communication of Hereditary Breast and Ovarian Cancer Genetic Information in Italian Women: Towards a Personalised Approach." *European Journal of Human Genetics*, 29(2), 250–261. https://www.nature.com/articles/s41431-020-00723-7.

8. Scarduzio, Real, Slone, and Henning 2018. "Vocational Anticipatory Socialization, Self-Determination Theory, and Meaningful Work."

9. Holman and Koenig Kellas 2018. "'Say something instead of nothing.'"

10. Rubinsky and Cooke-Jackson. "'Tell me something other than to use a condom and sex is scary.'"

11. Rubinsky and Cooke-Jackson 2017. "'Where is the love?'"

12. Rubinsky, Hosek, and Hudak 2019. "'It's better to be depressed skinny than happy fat.'"

13. Kim, I., B. Feng, J. Jang, and B. Wang. 2019. "Reassessing the Integrated Model of Advice-Giving in Supportive Interactions: The Moderating Roles of Need for Cognition and Communication Styles." *Social Influence*, 14(1), 14–24. https://doi.org/10.1080/15534510.2019.1581083.

14. Guntzviller, L.M. 2018. "Advice Messages and Interactions." In *The Oxford Handbook of Advice*, edited by E.L. MacGeorge and L.M. Van Swol. Oxford University Press.

15. MacGeorge, E.L., L.M. Guntzviller, K.S. Brisini, L.C. Bailey, S.K. Salmon, K. Severen, and R.D. Cummings. 2017. "The Influence of Emotional Support Quality on Advice Evaluation and Outcomes." *Communication Quarterly*, 65(1), 80–96. https://doi.org/10.1080/01463373.2016.1176945.

16. MacGeorge, E.L., B. Feng, and B.R. Burleson. 2011. "Supportive Communication." In *Handbook of Interpersonal Communication*, edited by J.A. Daly and M.L. Knapp. Sage.

17. Bodie, G.D., S.M. Jones, M. Brinberg, A.M. Joyer, D.H. Solomon, and N. Ram. 2021. "Discovering the Fabric of Supportive Conversations: A Typology of Speaking Turns and Their Contingencies." *Journal of Language and Social Psychology*, 40(2), 214–237. https://doi.org/10.1177/0261927X20953604.

18. Dailey, R.M., L. LeFebvre, B. Crook, and N. Brody. 2016. "Relational Uncertainty and Communication in On-Again/Off-Again Romantic Relationships: Assessing Changes and Patterns across Recalled Turning Points." *Western Journal of Communication*, 80(3), 239–263. http://doi.org/10.1080/10570314.2015.1094123.

19. Brown, B. 2020. "Tarana Burke on Being Heard and Seen." https://brenebrown.com/podcast/brene-tarana-burke-on-empathy/.

20. Goldsmith, D.J. 2008. "Politeness Theory." In *Engaging Theories in Interpersonal Communication: Multiple perspectives*, edited by L.A. Baxter and D.O. Braithwaiet. Sage.

21. Willer, E.K., and J. Soliz. 2010. "Face Needs, Intragroup Status, and Women's Reactions to Socially Aggressive Face Threats." *Personal Relationships*, 17(4), 557–571. https://doi.org/10.1111/j.1475-6811.2010.01297.x.

22. Goldsmith, D.J. 2000. "Soliciting Advice: The Role of Sequential Placement in Mitigating Face Threat." *Communications Monographs*, 67(1), 1–19. https://doi.org/10.1080/03637750009376492.

23. Goldsmith. "Soliciting advice."

24. Holman and Koenig Kellas 2018. "'Say something instead of nothing.'"

25. Rubinsky and Cooke-Jackson. "'Tell me something other than to use a condom and sex is scary.'"

26. Rubinsky, V., and A. Cooke-Jackson. 2021. "'It would be nice to know I'm allowed to exist': Designing Ideal Familial Adolescent Messages for LGBTQ Women's Sexual Health." *American Journal of Sexuality Education*, 16(2), 221–237.

27. Cairns, P., I. Pinker, A. Ward, E. Watson, and A. Laidlaw. 2021. "Empathy Maps in Communication Skills Training." *The Clinical Teacher*, 18(2), 142–146. https://doi.org/10.1111/tct.13270.

Further Reading

Brown, B. 2020. *Atlas of the Heart: Mapping Meaningful Connection and the Language of Human Experience.* Random House.

Cooke-Jackson, A., and V. Rubinsky. 2018. "Deeply Rooted in Memories: Toward a Comprehensive Overview of 30 Years of Memorable Message Literature." *Health Communication, 33*(4), 409–422. https://doi.org/10.1080/10410236.2016.1278491.

Cooke-Jackson, A. and V. Rubinsky (eds.). 2021. *Communicating Intimate Health.* Rowman & Littlefield.

Cooke-Jackson, A., and V. Rubinsky. 2021. "Theory of Memorable Messages." In *Communicating Intimate Health,* edited by A. Cooke-Jackson & V. Rubinsky. Rowman & Littlefield.

Cooke-Jackson, A., and V. Rubinsky. 2023. "Extending the Roots of Memorable Messages: A Comprehensive Review and Forecast of Memorable Message Literature and Theory." *Health Communication, 38*(12), 2676–2686. https://doi.org/10.1080/10410236.2022.2105620.

Gunning, J.N., and C. Taladay-Carter. 2024. "Grieving 'The Death of Possibility': Memorable Messages of (Dis) Enfranchised Loss in Invisible, Physical Illness." *Health Communication, 39*(10), 2152–2162. https://doi.org/10.1080/10410236.2023.2257942.

Horstman, H.K., E. Jordan, and J. Yue. 2023. "Memorable Messages in Families." In *Oxford Research Encyclopedia of Communication.* https://doi.org/10.1080/10410236.2021.1973718.

Horstman, H.K., Morrison, S., M.C. McBride, and A. Holman. 2023. "Memorable Messages Embedded in Men's Stories of Miscarriage: Extending Communicated Narrative Sense-Making and Memorable Message Theorizing." *Health Communication, 38*(4), 742–752.

Kaufmann, R., J.I. Vallade, and B.N. Frisby. 2021. "Memorable Messages in Times of Uncertainty: Communicative Strategies to Encourage Motivation and Connection." *Communication Education, 70*(3), 288–306. https://doi.org/10.1080/03634523.2021.1904144.

Kellas, J.K., T. Morgan, C. Taladay, M. Minton, J. Forte, and E. Husmann. 2020. "Narrative Connection: Applying CNSM Theory's Translational Storytelling Heuristic." *Journal of Family Communication, 20*(4), 360–376. https://doi.org/10.1080/15267431.2020.1826485.

Kuang, K., Z. Tian, S.R. Wilson, and P.M. Buzzanell. 2023. "Memorable Messages as Anticipatory Resilience: Examining Associations Among Memorable Messages, Communication Resilience Processes, and Mental Health." *Health Communication,* 38(6), 1136–1145. https://doi.org/10.1080/10410236.2021.1993585.

MacGeorge, E.L., B. Feng, and E.R. Thompson. 2008. "'Good' and 'Bad' Advice." In *Studies in Applied Interpersonal Communication,* edited by M. Motley. Sage.

Merolla, A.J., G.A. Beck, and A. Jones. 2017. "Memorable Messages as Sources of Hope." *Communication Quarterly,* 65(4), 456–480. https://doi.org/10.1080/01463373.2017.1288149.

Smith, S., and J. Butler Ellis. 2001. "Memorable Messages as Guides to Self-Assessment of Behavior: An Initial Investigation." *Communication Monographs*, 68(2), 154–168. https://doi.org/10.1080/03637750128058.

Stohl, C. 1986. "The Role of Memorable Messages in the Process of Organizational Socialization." *Communication Quarterly*, 34(3), 231–249 https://doi.org/10.1080/01463378609369638.

Index

www.ingramcontent.com/pod-product-compliance
Lightning Source LLC
Chambersburg PA
CBHW070038100426
42740CB00013B/2718

9781476698960